WEED:
GROW IT, COOK IT

FLOYD BARRINGTON

DOG 'n' BONE

Published in 2015 by Dog 'n' Bone Books
An imprint of Ryland Peters & Small Ltd

20–21 Jockey's Fields   341 E 116th St
London WC1R 4BW   New York, NY 10029

www.rylandpeters.com

10 9 8 7 6 5 4 3 2 1

Text © Floyd Barrington 2015
Design and illustration © Dog 'n' Bone Books 2015

A CIP catalog record for this book is available from the Library of Congress and the British Library.

ISBN: 978 1 909313 57 6

Printed in China

Editor: Clare Sayer
Style illustration: John Riordan
Step illustration: Dan Prange
Picture credits: Thanks to the following for the images on pages 52–54:
Aphid: Alvesgaspar; Fungus Gnat: James Lindsey at Ecology of Commanster; Spotted Spider Mite: J. Holopainen; Thrip: OpenCage; White Fly: Gaucho; Leaf Miner: N3v3rl4nd

CONTENTS

GROW IT

COOK IT

INTRODUCTION

WARNING: GROWING WEED IS HIGHLY ADDICTIVE!

It is well known that smoking and eating cannabis is not addictive. What most people don't realize is that growing it is incredibly so. The moment you germinate that first little seed you will be hooked for life. As a hobby, it's very easy and surprisingly inexpensive to get into, plus it's also hugely rewarding; for less than you would typically spend on an ounce or two of weed you can build a basic indoor setup capable of yielding a pound or more in just a few months.

This book aims to make growing weed as easy as possible by presenting all the essential information in a way that even the most stoned mind can understand. At first some of the charts and the scientific stuff might seem like a lot to take in (especially if you've had a smoke before you get started!), but don't panic, everything is more simple than it might appear at first. Just follow the advice here and you'll soon achieve great results. There will be problems and disappointments along the way, but you will learn from them. Growing weed is very much a case of the more you put in (both in time and money) the more you get out. Fortunately, once you start growing you won't be able to stop!

As well as growing weed, this book will show you how to harvest your crop, make very potent hash, and make canna-butter/oil, which can be used in the recipes for some cannabis-infused culinary delights (see pages 68–79). So get your gardening gloves and chef's hat at the ready and give growing and cooking weed a try.

A BRIEF HISTORY

If you thought weed was just about getting stoned with your mates, you'd be wrong—there's a lot more to it than that...

Mankind's relationship with cannabis can be traced back about ten millennia to the end of the last ice age. This was an era known as the Neolithic Revolution—a time when people abandoned their nomadic lifestyle in favor of settling in one place where the focus was on farming rather than hunting and gathering. Around this time people were migrating into northern Asia from Africa. Luckily for us, this happened to be the home of the cannabis plant, and people were quick to make the most of this new miracle crop. Its versatility and ease of cultivation would make it one of the most important substances and most widely grown crops in human history.

Many cultures have used cannabis for manufacturing everything from rope, textiles, and paper to fuel, food, and even building materials. Of course, our ancestors also made the most of its medicinal and curative effects. It has been widely used throughout the ages for recreation, human bonding, and spiritual enlightenment. Although the industrial and medicinal use of cannabis has been greatly suppressed over the last century, many people are now rediscovering its multitude of benefits.

It has been estimated that over 50,000 products can be manufactured from the cannabis plant, including building composites and plastics. The chemicals in cannabis can treat over 250 diseases and illnesses plus a long list of other ailments, making it a potential treatment for more conditions than any other substance. Its potential is so great that some believe it could actually stop wars, save the environment, boost economies, and improve the general health and wellbeing of humankind. So next time you're having a smoke, raise a joint in appreciation of 10,000 years of stoner history.

SATIVA, INDICA, AND RUDERALIS

So, what actually is it that you've been grinding up and rolling in your joints all these years? The first person to classify weed officially was Carolus Linnaeus, the Swedish botanist who devised the modern system for naming species. In 1753, using samples of European hemp that was widely cultivated at the time, Linnaeus named the plant *Cannabis sativa* L., "sativa" coming from the Latin word for "cultivated" and the "L" standing for Linnaeus (one of the conventions of the naming system). He considered it to be monotypic (having just one species) and believed it had originated in northern India. However, research in the 1930s by the Russian botanist Nicolai Vavilov identified it as originating in the Samarkand area north of Afghanistan and the Hindu Kush mountains.

In 1785 the French biologist Jean-Baptiste de Lamarck suggested that it was actually polytypic (having more than one species). His studies revealed differences between the European hemp and samples he had collected on his travels through India (a bit like many backpackers do today!) These plants varied enough to be classed as a distinct separate species, which he named *Cannabis indica* Lam. ("indica" representing its Indian heritage).

In 1924, almost 150 years after Lamarck's discovery, the Russian botanist D.E. Janichevsky was studying feral cannabis along the Volga River in Western Siberia and concluded that there was actually a third species. He called it *Cannabis ruderalis* Janisch., from the Latin word "*rudus*," meaning rubble—ruderal species of plants being those that first emerge from freshly disturbed ground.

How to tell cannabis plants apart by leaf shape

SATIVA

INDICA

RUDERALIS

In 1976, Canadian botanist Ernest Small and American taxonomist Arthur Cronquist suggested that the divergence between indicas and sativas was a result of human selection and cultivation, sativa being well suited to fiber and seed production and indica being used primarily for drug production.

This was backed up in studies also from the 1970s, by professors William Emboden and Loran Anderson, and Harvard botanist Richard E. Schultes. They concluded that there were indeed physical traits sufficiently different for cannabis to be categorized into the three separate species. The more widespread sativas, growing tall and sparingly branched with narrow leaflets, were normally found in warm lowland regions. Indicas, being shorter and bushier with wider leaflets, were adapted to cooler climates and highland regions, while the branchless ruderalis, being the shortest of the three, was found growing wild in Europe and central Asia.

You might think, "Why is this important to me?" Well, my green-fingered apprentice, read on...

How to tell cannabis plants apart by shape and size

SATIVA   INDICA   RUDERALIS

THE SCIENCE

Cannabis is a highly versatile and adaptable annual flowering herb capable of thriving at altitudes of up to 8,000 feet (2,438m). It has a life cycle of three to six months and can grow at a rate of 6in (15cm) a day (although 1–2in/2–5cm is typical). Some varieties can mature as small as 12in (30cm) while others may stretch to 20 feet (6m) and beyond—about the size of your average two-story house.

Cannabis plants are dioecious, which means they will be either male or female—male flowers produce pollen and females make the seeds. Both male and female plants have glands that secrete a sticky resin, although the females produce much more. These glands, called "trichomes," are most prevalent on the flowers, which if left unpollinated will continue to swell and grow, forming large columns of resin-coated buds known as "colas." This resin contains chemicals such as Delta-9-Tetrahydrocannabinol (THC) and Cannabidiol (CBD), known collectively as "cannabinoids." These chemicals are responsible for the mental and physical effects that a user experiences. In other words, they are the stuff that gets you baked.

These cannabinoids work by interacting with cannabinoid receptors in the brain and indirectly increasing the levels of a neurotransmitter called dopamine (neurotransmitters are chemicals that occur naturally in the brain and are used to transmit information and send messages to the body). When dopamine is released, it makes a person feel good, and at these increased levels it produces the psychoactive (or mashed) effects that you are no doubt familiar with.

The type of cannabis you use can have a significant impact on the effect experienced. THC produces the uplifting, cerebral "high" that a user experiences, while higher CBD levels can lead to an increase in the physically relaxing "stoned" feeling (a characteristic favored by many medicinal users). Additionally, higher levels of another cannabinoid called cannabinol (CBN) can lead to increased uneasiness, anxiety, and disorientation. If you've ever thrown a whitey, you'll be all too familiar with these effects.

Indica strains were developed throughout history primarily for cannabis's medicinal benefits. As such they now typically have higher proportions of CBD than sativa strains. This makes indica strains generally more relaxing, providing a "body stone" ideal for chilling out in the evening, while sativas give more of an energetic and euphoric high—perfect for daytime smoking when you need to get stuff done.

The colorful world of weed

MODERN CULTIVATION

You've had the history and science lessons, now it's time to learn how weed and the culture surrounding it have evolved in recent times.

Before the 1960s the vast majority, if not all, of cannabis consumed in Western Europe and North America was imported and generally differentiated by its country of origin. In the early 1960s large-scale importation of weed and hash was rapidly increasing. Most of the weed smuggled at that time was produced from sativa strains and contained seeds. However, these seeds gave people the opportunity to experiment with growing their own, especially in tropical areas such as Florida and California. By the late 1960s certain strains, such as Panama Red and Acapulco Gold, had gained legendary status.

In the early 1970s growers began producing weed without seeds, known as sinsemilla, from the Spanish sin meaning "without" and semilla meaning "seeds." This was achieved by removing male plants to prevent the female plants from being pollinated. This causes the females to put all their energy into making big, swollen, resin-rich flower buds instead of seeds—resulting in a higher-grade product.

By the mid-1970s sinsemilla was the leading type of domestically grown cannabis. Cultivators soon began developing strains suited for indoor growing under artificial lights, allowing them to control the heat and light and in turn increase the potency and yield of their plants. Cross-pollination then led to selective breeding of plants for particular traits such as flavor, smell, or color. Further crossbreeding and inbreeding eventually resulted in some of the famous sativa strains of the 1970s, such as Purple Haze, Maui Wowie, and Eden Gold.

The mid- to late 1970s also saw the introduction of indica strains to Europe and North America from Central Asia and the Middle East. These shorter, bushier, and earlier-maturing plants soon became popular as they were easier to hide, often more potent, and usually more cost-effective for the grower than their sativa cousins. It wasn't long before breeders were cross-pollinating sativa and indica strains to create plants with the bushy, early-maturing, and potent traits of the indica but with the more uplifting high of the sativa strains.

By the 1980s cultivation of sinsemilla had become more common, and the vast majority of plants grown had traces of both sativa and indica genetics. Owing to political pressure on US growers and a more relaxed view in the Netherlands, the reins of the cannabis-breeding industry were passed from the Californians to the Dutch. With advances

in growing techniques and a better understanding of the plant, the Dutch breeders went on to make some of the most famous strains known today, and established themselves as the leaders in cannabis cultivation. Although it must be noted that almost all the Dutch varieties owe their genetic heritage to a handful of the North American strains grown in the 1960s and 1970s.

In the mid-1990s, the attitude of the Dutch authorities began to change, and stricter limits were put in place for the coffee shops. Meanwhile, the opposite was happening across the pond. In 1996, California enacted Proposition 215, allowing the medicinal use of cannabis, and this was followed over the next few years with similar laws in Oregon, Maine, Nevada, and Colorado.

The twenty-first century saw increasing pressure on the Dutch, with many coffee shops being shut down. However, the pro-cannabis sentiment in the US was increasing. Laws for medicinal use or decriminalization were introduced across numerous states, and in 2012 recreational use was legalized in Colorado and Washington, with other states to follow. This dramatic overhaul of the legal landscape meant that the US was now back in the driving seat, propelling the science and business of cannabis forward to become the multi-billion-dollar industry that it always had the potential to be.

PLANT GENDER

And now it's time for a bit of sex education. As mentioned earlier, cannabis plants are dioecious, meaning that they are either male or female. However there are occasionally plants that are monoecious, bearing both male and female flowers, known as hermaphrodites. Sometimes female plants can even become hermaphroditic when subjected to stress, such as from a lighting failure or physical damage, so be sure to treat your ladies with respect.

So, how can you tell if your plant is a guy or a girl? Well, at around six to eight weeks old a plant will begin to show pre-flowers, which look like single regular flowers, consisting of a small green pod (calyx). These can be found at the branch internodes (the point where the branch meets the stem) just behind the leaf stipule (the small spur at the base of the branch). Female pre-flowers can be determined by a pair of white hair-like pistils emerging from the calyx, while male pre-flowers do not develop these.

How to identify the sex of cannabis pre-flowers

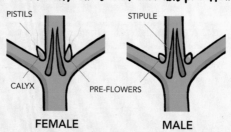

When genders have been established, remove any males from the crop. This stops females from becoming pollinated, allowing them to grow large, swollen flower buds. Once pre-flowering has started, plants are mature enough to be triggered into flowering by switching the light cycle (see page 18). You can keep them in a vegetative state for longer if you wish, but never switch before pre-flowering as the stress can produce hermaphrodites, which can pollinate themselves and other plants in a grow room. Once the light cycle is changed, growth slows and things start to get interesting, as flowering will be visible within a couple of weeks. Male plants are taller with fewer leaves, and tend to flower before females. Male flowers resemble miniature bunches of bananas or coconuts that hang from the plant and release a cloud of pollen, which is carried by the wind to the females.

Female flowers consist of a calyx, containing an ovule out of which emerges a pair of pistils. As she matures, more calyxes develop and swell into large, densely packed buds covered in THC, and the pistils darken to orange, red, or brown. If a female is pollinated, bud growth slows up and just one seed will develop in each calyx. The seeds contain almost no THC, which is why you don't want plants to be pollinated.

How to identify the Sex of cannabis flowers

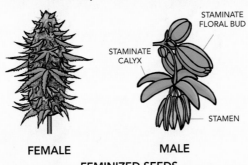

STAMINATE
FLORAL BUD

STAMINATE
CALYX

STAMEN

FEMALE   **MALE**

FEMINIZED SEEDS

Regular cannabis seeds will typically produce a 50/50 ratio of male to female plants. For some growers, especially those with a restricted grow space, growing double the number of plants that they ultimately want is impractical. Fortunately it is now possible to get feminized seeds, which produce female plants 90 percent or more of the time.

AUTOFLOWERING

Not everyone has access to huge, isolated outhouses in which to grow massive trees of weed. For many of us space is at a premium, particularly when you need to keep your crop under wraps. In such circumstances time is usually an issue too: the quicker you can harvest your plants, the less chance of your grow operation being discovered. That's where "autoflowering" plants come in handy.

Sativa and indica strains of cannabis are triggered into flowering when the amount of light and dark in a day reaches a certain level, around 12 hours of each. However, the shorter, lower-strength ruderalis varieties (see page 6) begin to flower at a certain age, regardless of light levels, and this trait has been successfully exploited in the development of autoflowering strains.

In the 1970s the Canadian botanist Ernest Small tried crossing ruderalis with more potent strains to make a plant that was compact and autoflowering, but still packed a punch. Unfortunately, the results were only partially successful—while compact and autoflowering, the plant contained only intermediate levels of THC. In the 1980s, Small's early work inspired Australian-born Nevil Schoenmakers, the "father of Dutch seed banks," to experiment with crossing ruderalis with more potent strains such as Skunk #1 and Northern Lights, but again the potency wasn't what he had hoped for.

Thankfully for stealth growers, in the late 1990s the true champion of ruderalis announced himself to the world: a Canadian known only as the Joint Doctor. While living on a farm in Quebec, the Doctor was given a cannabis seed by a Mexican friend, Antonio, who had been cultivating cannabis for many years. The seed was from a strain called Mexican Rudy, one that stayed short and flowered very early but was of medium potency. It is believed that it had been produced at an American university during the 1970s by crossing Mexican cannabis with Russian ruderalis (hence the name Mexican Rudy).

The Joint Doctor grew the Mexican Rudy and proceeded to cross it with other strains: first a cross with Northern Lights, then the resulting offspring crossed with a William's Wonder clone. This hybrid, initially dubbed William's Automatic, would go on to be known famously as Lowryder. This strain matured automatically at no more than 12 inches (30cm) and in less than 60 days from seed. Further crossbreeding of the Lowryder has now led to autoflowering strains that are as potent as many of the top traditional varieties. It is now even possible to get feminized autoflowering seeds, which provide the benefits of small plants, a quick harvest, and no unwanted males. What more could you ask for?

THAT'S DOPE: where to buy seeds

Cannabis seeds are available from seed banks, many of which can be found online. It is said that the first seed bank was started in California in the 1960s by a group called the Sacred Seed Collective. In 1985, a member called David Watson (AKA Skunk Man Sam) moved to Amsterdam, taking with him seeds of some legendary strains. He soon met three breeders, to whom he gave the seeds: Ben Dronkers, Eddie Reekeder, and Nevil Schoenmaekers, owner of the Seed Bank of Holland. Over the next decade they crossbred the seeds and produced some of the most famous strains around. Eddie went on to start the Flying Dutchmen Seed Bank and Ben the Sensi Seed Club. In 1991, Ben bought Nevil's company and formed the Sensi Seed Bank, then in 2006 he bought the Flying Dutchmen, giving the Sensi Seed Bank one of the best catalogs of weed strains available today.

INDOOR GROWING

Now you're familiar with the background of this amazing plant, it's finally time to start planning your grow room. But before you start setting things up, it's worth considering the following factors:

SOIL OR HYDROPONICS: This is the first decision you need to make. The type of setup will have an impact on the grow room you choose. If using hydroponics, consider any extra space needed to accommodate reservoirs and other equipment (see page 24).

SPACE: A grow room should be a self-contained space adequate for the number of plants you plan on growing. You might have an entire room available or just a small cupboard under the stairs—both will do the job perfectly well. Specially designed grow tents (right) are a good shout; these handy units come in a range of sizes and have built-in vents and fittings for all your equipment.

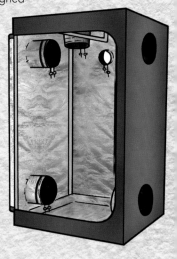

Giving your plants plenty of space is vital; they need to be able to grow freely with room around them for airflow and light penetration. An ideal grow space should be at least 6 feet (1.8m) tall and allow at least 1ft^2 (30cm^2) of space per plant, although the more the better. You can successfully grow in a tiny space, just consider the various methods of training (see page 48) or using autoflowering varieties (see page 14), which can mature at just 1 foot (30cm).

LIGHT: You want light to be able to reach all around your plants, so cover the walls with a reflective material such as Mylar® or simply paint the walls white. Do not use aluminum foil, as this can heat up and burn plants. Light escaping from a grow room is one way of getting busted, so ensure there are no leakages. It is also important that no light can get into your grow room during dark hours. See page 18 for more information on lighting.

HEAT: This can be a problem in small spaces. Make sure the surrounding area is not prone to extremes in temperature. When the lights go out the temperature can decrease dramatically, and cold temperatures are as much of a threat as high ones. Cops have also been known to use heat maps to detect grow operations. So maintaining a typical room temperature (68–79°F/20–26°C) in the surrounding area is important, especially if growing in a loft. See page 38 for more about temperature.

AIR SUPPLY AND ODOR CONTROL: To control heat and keep your plants happy, a grow room needs a supply of fresh air and a route for the old air to escape through. For fairly small spaces, a room with a window should be fine. Your area should also be as airtight as possible to contain any odors—you don't want the wrong people smelling out your stash. See page 20 for more about ventilation.

WATER: Like me and you, plants get thirsty and want a good drink from time to time. You will need constant access to water and a way to dispose of any unwanted liquids, so make sure these aren't too far away. Nobody wants to be lugging heavy buckets up three flights of stairs each time your plants need watering. Also, if using hydroponics, you will need to take precautions to avoid any floods or spills.

NOISE: Fans echoing through ducting can get noisy and get you caught (plus the sound will do your head in!), so locate your grow area away from anywhere it could easily be heard. Acoustic ducting and ventilation silencers can be used to reduce any noise.

CLEANLINESS: Pests and diseases thrive in dirty conditions, so maintain a high level of cleanliness both in your grow room and in the surrounding area. Do not have carpets or other surfaces in your grow area that can't be washed clean.

SAFETY: Water and electricity do not mix! Any grow area has lots of both, so be sensible. Keeping all electrical equipment and cables high up is a good way to avoid accidents.

SECURITY: People get caught because of laziness, complacency, or greed. Don't cut corners, make assumptions, or take unnecessary risks. Always think one step ahead, be constantly vigilant, and do not trust anyone.

LIGHTING

Nope, this isn't about the age-old issue of where you last saw that box of matches. This is a key element of growing weed that you don't want to be in the dark about.

With the exception of autoflowering strains, cannabis plants are photoperiodic, which means they begin to flower when the balance of light and dark reaches around 12 hours of each. At the start of your grow, use an electric plug timer to give your plants 18 hours of light per day to keep them in their vegetative growth stage.

When they finally get to the size you want, trigger the flowering stage by switching the light cycle to 12/12. (During flowering, a plant will usually double in size, so bear in mind how much space you have in your grow area before reducing the hours of light.) Autoflowering strains should be given around 18–20 hours of light per day throughout the entire life cycle.

> The color spectrum of the light will have an impact on your plants. The blue spectrum simulates the light of spring and is suited to vegetative growth, while the red spectrum, simulating summer light, is better for the flowering stage.

TYPES OF LIGHTING

High Intensity Discharge (HID): These are the most common lights used for growing weed. They are either metal halide (MH) or high-pressure sodium (HPS), intended for the vegetative and flowering stages respectively owing to the spectrum of light emitted.

When buying HID bulbs you will also need to buy a ballast (which limits the current supplied), a contactor (used for safe automatic switching), and a reflector or hood. HID bulbs produce a lot of heat, so air-cooled hoods are often used as these have their own independent ventilation. HID lights are available in a range of sizes—use a minimum of 30W/ft^2 for vegetative growth and 50W for flowering. The table opposite details the different wattages of HID bulbs available.

How to choose HID lighting for your grow room

Wattage	Coverage Area	Distance from Plants
150W	2ft^2 (0.6m^2)	4–11in (10–28cm)
250W	2–2.5ft^2 (0.6–0.8m^2)	5–13in (13–33cm)
400W	3–3.5ft^2 (0.9–1m^2)	6–19in (15–48cm)
600W	3.5–4ft^2 (1–1.2m^2)	8–25in (20–64cm)
1000W	4–5ft^2 (1.2–1.5m^2)	10–31in (26–79cm)

Compact Fluorescent Light (CFL): CFLs use less electricity than HID lights but are not as effective, with the light only being useful up to a distance of 2 feet (60cm). However, it is still possible to get decent results with CFLs, especially with short plants in small grow spaces. CFLs don't give out as much heat as HID lights, so they can be positioned closer to the plants and require considerably less ventilation. They are often used for seedlings and clones, so if you start with CFLs and move onto HID lights you will still be able to make use of them.

It is recommended to have a minimum of 45W/ft^2 for vegetative growth and 65W/ft^2 for flowering. The best for vegetative growth are the "daylight" spectrum bulbs rated as 6500k, while the "warm white" (2700k) bulbs are best suited to flowering.

Light-emitting Diode (LED): The most efficient grow lighting, producing the least heat and lasting the longest of all grow lights. Unfortunately they are very expensive, and there are lots of badly made LED setups on the market, so be careful when making a purchase.

> You should hang the lights in your grow room in a way that allows them to be raised as your plants grow–chains or specially designed light hangings are ideal.

VENTILATION

Now it's time to take a deep breath and get ready for the exciting topic that is ventilation. Well, I say exciting, it's not quite as fun as rolling up a joint from your first crop of home grown, but setting up a good ventilation system is vital for a number of reasons: plants absorb carbon dioxide for photosynthesis; fresh air reduces humidity that can encourage diseases and pests; the movement caused by airflow helps to strengthen the plants; and air replenishment is needed to maintain optimal temperatures. Finally, ventilation can also reduce that telltale smell, so all in all it's a pretty important element to think about.

The basic principle for setting up a grow-room ventilation system is that there should be an intake of cool, fresh air and a route to exhaust old, warm air. Because hot air rises, the exhaust should be near the top of your grow room and the intake at the bottom. An inline fan is used to blow the air out of the exhaust (known as an active exhaust). Although fans can be used for the intake, it's generally okay just to have an opening (known as a passive intake). The intake should be a little smaller than the exhaust to create negative pressure in the room and prevent odors escaping through any other gaps.

Pushing air through a carbon filter

HOT AIR PULLED OUT

PASSIVE INTAKE

COLD AIR PULLED IN

HOT AIR BLOWN OUT OF FILTER

The air expelled by the fan can be pushed through a carbon filter to remove any odor. Alternatively, it can be pulled through the filter and then expelled through the fan. Inline fans are rated by the amount of air they pass in a given time, measured as cubic feet per minute (cfm) or meters cubed per hour (m^3/h). Ideally, the fan should replace the air in your room once every minute, although hot grow rooms, particularly those with HID lights, may need five or more exchanges per minute to keep the temperature under control.

Pulling air through a carbon filter

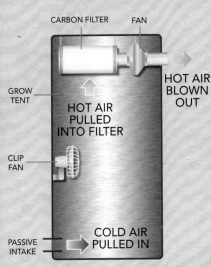

CARBON FILTER   FAN

GROW TENT

HOT AIR PULLED INTO FILTER

CLIP FAN

COLD AIR PULLED IN

PASSIVE INTAKE

HOT AIR BLOWN OUT

To calculate your required cfm rating, work out the volume of your room by multiplying the length by width by height (in feet). So the volume of a room 2 feet long by 2 feet wide by 6 feet high would be $2 \times 2 \times 6 = 24$ cubic feet. Therefore you need a fan rated at 24cfm or above. To calculate the m^3/h rating calculate the volume of your grow room (in meters) and multiply by 60.

Other factors will also have an impact on the airflow. For example, bends in ducting will reduce the flow by around 5–10 percent. If adding a carbon filter, you should increase the fan rating by about 25 percent. In addition to the ventilation fan, it is also necessary to have one or more fans circulating the air inside the grow room. Clip-on desk fans should do the job.

For very small stealth grows, inline fans and carbon filters may not always be needed. PC fans can be a great alternative for small projects. If you are still concerned about the smell, there are tubs of odor-absorbing gel available from grow shops and online that can be placed in a grow room.

GROWING MEDIUMS

All growing mediums have their advantages and disadvantages. Some people argue that the only way to go is hydro, while others swear on their mother's life that soil grows are the best. My advice: try them all yourself to see which best fits your needs.

Soil is the most common and easily accessible for beginners, but as you hone your skills, you will possibly find that the flexibility and control offered by the hydroponic substances make them a better choice.

SOIL: Soil can consist of rock, sand, clay, moss, and other organic materials. It also contains microorganisms that break down organic material and are essential in providing soil with its life-giving properties. Most commercial soils will also have added fertilizers. When buying soils you need to consider the NPK values (see page 44). Use seedling compost for young plants, as they are particularly sensitive to nutrient burn.

Soil is a smart choice for first-timers—it's cheap and fairly easy to maintain, and there is much less need to test the pH than with a hydroponic setup. On the downside, soil encourages pests and diseases, and it is more difficult to flush if there is a nutritional or chemical problem. Drainage is another common problem, so be careful not to under- or overwater. If using soil, mix it with about 25 percent perlite, to help with water retention and drainage.

> Never use soil from your garden, unless you are planting outside, as it contains pests and diseases. Even if you are growing outside, you are better off filling a hole with fresh soil or a mixture of old and new.

COCO COIR: This is an eco-friendly by-product of coconut processing. It is highly aerated, encouraging roots to grow to their full potential, and is completely inert, meaning that it has no nutritional properties. It can be used in hydroponic setups or as you would soil. Coco coir has naturally occurring rooting hormones to promote healthy root growth, and offers higher resistance to fungal infections and root disease than other mediums. Coco coir does tend to absorb calcium and magnesium, so use a cal/mag supplement.

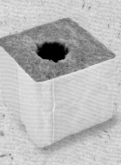

ROCKWOOL: This is a lightweight, inert hydroponic medium with excellent water-retention properties. Resembling loft insulation, it is made by spinning molten rock into fibers, which are then formed into cubes and slabs of various sizes. A good size cube for seedlings and cuttings is 1½in (36mm), before moving on to another growing medium or larger cubes. It has a high pH, so before use it should be soaked in water with a pH of 5.6 for several hours.

EXPANDED CLAY PEBBLES: This is an ecologically sustainable growing medium, made from porous clay pebbles that are ideal for hydroponic grows. They are inert and pH neutral, but wash them before use to remove dust. They are pricier than other mediums, but can be reused, saving you money in the long run.

PERLITE: Made by heat-expanding volcanic glass, these highly absorbent granules are inert and pH neutral. They are usually combined with other growing mediums to aid water retention and drainage, but can also be used on their own. They contain a lot of dust, so rinse well before use and never use in a recovery hydroponic system (one that recycles the excess fluids) in case it gets drawn into the pump. Vermiculite is similar to perlite and can be used instead.

HYDROPONIC BASICS

For newbie growers, hydroponics might look more suited to a NASA laboratory than a closet grow room, but it's actually a lot simpler than it may seem at first.

Hydroponic setups use a nutrient solution in water and, instead of soil, plants are grown in a water-retaining medium (see page 22). The first benefit of hydroponics is that the roots are provided with a lot of oxygen, often with the aid of an air pump. Secondly, the nutrients are more abundant than in soil and under conditions that make them easier to absorb, resulting in larger plants that grow faster. Hydroponic solutions are also less susceptible to infection from pests and diseases. Below are the six main types of hydroponic system.

WICK SYSTEM:

This is the simplest method. Nutrient solution is drawn up a wick from a reservoir and into the growing medium. An air pump, connected to an air stone, is put into the reservoir to aerate the solution.

GROWING MEDIUM

RESERVOIR

WICK

AIR STONE

GROW TRAY

AIR PUMP

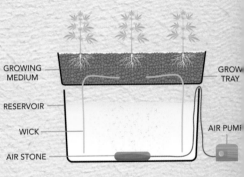

DRIP MANIFOLD

DRIP LINE

OVERFLOW DRAIN PIPE

NUTRIENT PUMP

DRIP SYSTEM:

A timer-controlled pump in the reservoir pumps nutrient solution up to a drip line, dripping it onto the base of the plants. Some systems collect the excess run-off solution back into the reservoir—this is known as a recovery system.

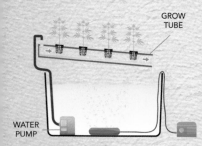

FLOATING
PLATFORM

NET POT

DEEP WATER CULTURE (DWC):
A deep reservoir is filled with nutrient solution and net pots are floated on the surface using a foam raft, or are suspended just above the solution, with only the roots outside the pots being submerged (see DIY DWC on page 26).

EBB AND FLOW (AKA FLOOD AND DRAIN):
A submerged water pump, controlled by a timer, pumps nutrient solution from the reservoir into the grow tray. Once the tray is flooded the pump switches off and the solution drains back into the reservoir. This is repeated every few hours or so.

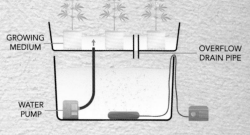

GROWING
MEDIUM

OVERFLOW
DRAIN PIPE

WATER
PUMP

GROW
TUBE

WATER
PUMP

NUTRIENT FILM TECHNIQUE (NFT):
The nutrient solution is pumped into a downward-sloping tube so that a shallow film of solution flows down it. The plants are suspended through the tube with the roots hanging down, touching the passing solution.

AEROPONIC: In this system the roots are suspended in air and misted with a spray of nutrient solution every couple of minutes.

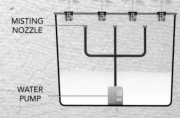

MISTING
NOZZLE

WATER
PUMP

DIY DEEP-WATER CULTURE SYSTEM

So you want to try hydroponics? Well, a homemade DWC system is the perfect place to start. This guide explains how to make a bucket system to fit a single plant, but the same principles, along with a larger container, can be used to make a multiple plant system. You'll be swimming in green in no time.

You will need:

- 4–5 gallon (20–25 liter) bucket with lid (ideally black or a dark color to prevent algae)
- Net pot: approximately 5in (14cm)
- Sharp knife
- Power drill with ¾in (19mm) and ³⁄₁₆in (5mm) drill bits
- Rubber grommet: ½in (13mm) inside; ¾in (19mm) outside
- ½in (13mm) 90-degree elbow connector
- ½in (13mm) clear tubing (ideally green or blue to prevent algae)
- Cable tie
- Strong glue or a hot glue gun
- Air stone
- ¼in (6mm) airline tubing (length will vary depending on distance from bucket to pump)
- Air pump rated at a minimum of 65gal/hr (300l/hr)
- Permanent marker pen

1 Mark out a circle in the center of the bucket lid, slightly smaller than the diameter of the net pot, and cut it out with a sharp knife. Make sure the pot fits snugly in the hole. It's best to cut the hole a little too small first and then adjust it, rather than making it too big.

2 Using the ¾in (19mm) drill bit, make a hole in the side of the bucket about ¾in (19mm) from the bottom. Insert the rubber grommet into the hole and insert the 90-degree elbow connector into the grommet. Using the ³⁄₁₆in (5mm) bit, drill a hole in the side of the bucket about 2in (50mm) from the top.

3 Cut a length of the ½in (13mm) tubing approximately 3in (75mm) shorter than the height of the bucket, and push one end onto the elbow connector. This will act as your water level indicator and a way to refill and empty the reservoir. Using the knife, make two small holes vertically in line with the elbow connector, approximately 4in (100mm) from the top of the bucket and about ½in (13mm) apart. Feed the cable tie through the holes to make a loop, which will keep the indicator tube held upright.

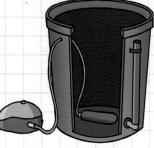

4 Using the glue, stick the air stone to the bottom of the bucket. Connect the airline tubing and pass it through the ³⁄₁₆in (5mm) hole (made in step 2). Connect the other end of the tubing to the air pump.

5 Now it's time to work out the water levels. Fill the bucket with water so that, when the lid is put on the bucket, the water level reaches about ½in (13mm) below the bottom of the net pot. Mark this level on the ½in (13mm) tubing with a permanent marker pen. This will be the level required when the roots have eventually grown through the net pot. Now add more water to the bucket so the water level reaches about ½in (13mm) above the bottom of the net pot. This will be the water level required before the roots have emerged.

6 Now, add your nutrients to the water, pot up your plant using clay pebbles, and switch on the air pump.

7 Use an EC meter to check the reservoir strength regularly and top up as needed (see page 46). Because the plant roots will be submerged in the nutrient solution, it is important that an optimum reservoir temperature of around 60-70°F (16-21°C) is maintained. You should also regularly check the pH (see page 40) and adjust as required, aiming for a pH of around 5.8.

DIY EBB AND FLOW HYDROPONIC SYSTEM

Now you've got your feet wet with a DWC system, here's something a bit more advanced to try. The ebb and flow system uses a water pump, but is still a simple project. The steps explain how to make a two-plant system, but could easily be adapted for any number.

You will need:

- A dark-colored plastic storage/ tote box with lid: approximately 20 gallons (100 liters) capacity
- ½in (13mm) clear tubing (ideally green or blue to prevent algae)
- Rubber grommet: ½in (13mm) inside; ¾in (19mm) outside
- ½in (13mm) 90-degree elbow connector
- Cable tie
- Plastic tray roughly the same length and width as the storage box but about a third as high (plastic cement-mixing trays work well, or you can cut down a second box)
- Power drill with 1¼in (32mm) hole saw and a ⅜in (10mm) drill bit, and a ¾in (19mm) drill bit
- ¾in (19mm) ebb and flow fitting set
- 20in (50cm) length of black irrigation tubing with ½in (13mm) inner diameter
- Submersible water pump rated at approximately 120gal/hr (600l/hr)

- Air stone
- ¼in (6mm) airline tubing (length will vary depending on distance from bucket to pump)
- Air pump rated at a minimum of 65gal/hr (300l/hr)
- Electrical plug timer
- 2 net pots: approximately 5in (14cm)
- Expanded clay pebbles

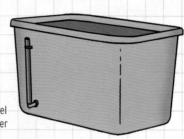

1 Use the clear tubing, grommet, elbow connector, and cable tie to make a level indicator tube as shown for the deep-water culture project (page 26).

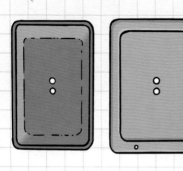

2 Cut two 1¼in (32mm) holes in the center of the plastic tray. Place the tray on top of the box lid, taking care to line it up so it is central. Mark the holes onto the tray before drilling them out too. With the ¾in (19mm) drill bit, cut another hole in the lid as shown.

3 Fit the ebb and flow fittings (left) into the holes of the tray.

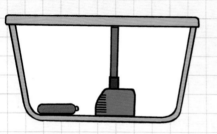

4 Attach the irrigation tubing to the water pump outlet and put it into the storage box. Trim the tubing so that the pump can sit on the bottom of the box with the tubing just meeting the lid when it is put on. Position the air stone inside the box.

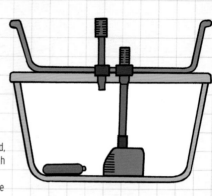

5 Put the tray on top of the lid, lining up the fittings through the lid holes. Now connect the irrigation tubing to the underside port of the inflow tube.

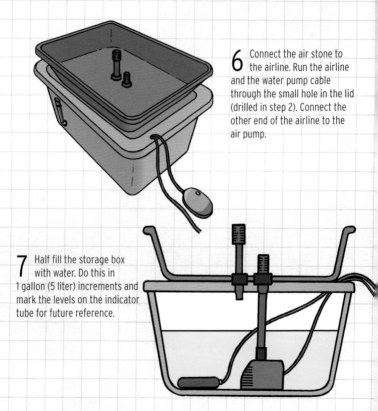

6 Connect the air stone to the airline. Run the airline and the water pump cable through the small hole in the lid (drilled in step 2). Connect the other end of the airline to the air pump.

7 Half fill the storage box with water. Do this in 1 gallon (5 liter) increments and mark the levels on the indicator tube for future reference.

8 Turn on the water pump. It will begin pumping water from the reservoir into the grow tray. When the water reaches the level of the overflow pipe it drains back into the reservoir. Use the timer to set the water pump to come on for 15 minutes, three times per day during the plant's light hours. Throughout the grow you may need to adjust the timing, especially in hot temperatures, when the growing medium will dry out quicker. The air pump should stay on permanently.

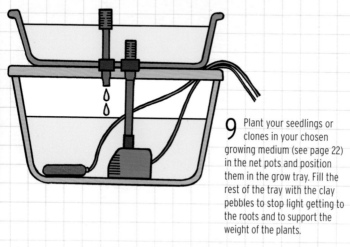

9 Plant your seedlings or clones in your chosen growing medium (see page 22) in the net pots and position them in the grow tray. Fill the rest of the tray with the clay pebbles to stop light getting to the roots and to support the weight of the plants.

10 Use an EC meter to check the reservoir strength regularly, and top up as needed (see page 46). Unlike with DWC systems, reservoir temperature is not as much of a concern in an ebb and flow setup. You should still regularly check the pH (see page 40) and adjust as required, aiming for a pH of around 5.8. Before you know it you'll have a pair of bud-smothered plants ready to be chopped down and enjoyed.

GERMINATING SEEDS

Some seeds are lazy little bastards and need a bit of encouragement. Rather than putting them straight into your growing medium, give your seeds a kickstart by sprouting them first using the method below.

1 Fold a few sheets of paper towel so they will fit into the container, and pour on some water so the towel becomes thoroughly wet but not drenched. Place the seeds on top of the towel and fold the wet paper over the top of them.

You will need:

- A small container with a lid, such as the plastic boxes from takeout restaurants
- Some paper towel
- A bottle of distilled or mineral water

2 Put the lid on the container and put it somewhere dark at a temperature of around 70–88°F (21–31°C). Check occasionally to make sure the paper towel hasn't dried out. After 24-72 hours the seeds will crack open and a white sprout called a radicle will pop out. This is the root or taproot.

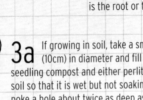

3a If growing in soil, take a small pot approximately 4in (10cm) in diameter and fill it with a 50/50 mixture of seedling compost and either perlite or vermiculite. Water the soil so that it is wet but not soaking. Use a pencil or similar to poke a hole about twice as deep as the length of the seed.

3b If you plan to grow hydroponically it's best to use rockwool starter cubes. Before use, soak the cubes for several hours in water adjusted to pH 5.5 (see page 40), then shake them to remove any excess water. Use a pencil or similar to open up the hole (or create a hole if there's not a pre-made one).

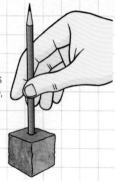

4 Gently place the seed into the hole with the sprout facing downward and cover with a thin layer of medium. Some growers choose not to pre-germinate, and instead put the unsprouted seed directly into the growing medium. If you choose this option ensure that you plant the seed with its pointed end facing down.

5 Place the pot or rockwool cube inside a propagator with a transparent cover. This will act like a small greenhouse keeping the air inside moist and warm—perfect for encouraging seedlings to grow. Put the propagator under suitable seedling lights (CFL lighting is ideal) for 18 hours per day, aiming for a temperature of around 70-77°F (21-25°C). To reduce the risk of mold, occasionally lift up the propagator cover to provide fresh air.

6 After a day or two the little seedling will finally make its way out of the soil, revealing a pair of tiny round leaves called cotyledons. As soon as it comes through, remove the pot or cube from the propagator. Leaving seedlings in humid conditions for too long can cause rotting or a fungal infection called "damping off." Keep the seedlings under the seedling lights for a few days before moving to more powerful lights. Cannabis seeds can be expensive, though, so turn the page for a way to get weed plants for free.

CLONING

This might evoke images of mad scientists, Dolly the Sheep, or a shit Michael Keaton film that I saw when I was mashed, but really it's just an old technique to replicate plants, commonly known as taking cuttings. All cannabis seeds are different, each producing plants with their own distinct characteristics. However, by taking a cutting, a plant can be cloned, creating a second plant with the same genetic makeup as the first. As such, it will have the same physical tendencies too (including gender, size, and flowering time). Therefore, many growers select plants from their crops that exhibit desirable characteristics and use them to make genetically identical clones. This method also eliminates unwanted males and is usually faster than starting from seed.

Cuttings should only ever be taken from a plant while it is in its vegetative stage (i.e. not while flowering), and cuttings taken from lower down are easier to root than those from high up. Also, nitrogen stored in the mother plant can inhibit rooting of the clones, so it's advisable to flush it first for around a week prior to taking cuttings (see page 40).

HOW TO TAKE CUTTINGS

You will need:
- Small pot of soil and perlite or rockwool cube
- Sharp blade
- Sterilizing agent/rubbing alcohol

- Rooting hormone (ideally a gel variety, but powder can be used)
- Propagator
- Spray bottle filled with dechlorinated water

1 If growing in soil, fill a small pot with a 50/50 mixture of seedling compost and perlite, and water thoroughly. If growing hydroponically, use a rockwool cube soaked overnight in pH 5.5-adjusted nutrient solution at a strength of around 350ppm (see chart on page 47), and shake off any excess water before use. Use a pencil or similar to make a hole in your growing medium about 1in (25mm) deep.

2 Cut off a side shoot from the mother plant approximately 2–4in (5–10cm) long with a new growth tip and at least one leaf internode, two if possible (a leaf internode is where a leaf connects to the stem).

3 Sterilize the blade and use it to carefully slice off the lower petioles (leaf stems) flush with the main stem. Now cleanly cut through the stem at a 45-degree angle, approximately ¼in (6mm) below the previous cuts.

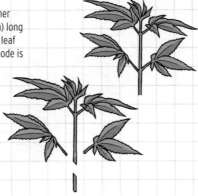

4 Immediately dip the stem into the rooting hormone, making sure it covers the cut parts of the stem. Get the stem into the rooting hormone as quickly as possible to avoid air entering the cut. Put the cutting into water if there's going to be a delay.

5 Now put the cutting into the soil or rockwool and gently pack down the medium around the stem, securing it in place. If the cutting has particularly large leaves you can trim them down slightly so the clone can focus its energy on rooting rather than supporting the extra vegetation.

6 Mist the inside of the propagator with water and place the cutting inside. Place it under suitable lighting for around 18 hours per day (CFL lighting is recommended). Every few hours, lift up the cover to supply fresh air. Until the cutting has grown roots it will be obtaining all its moisture through its leaves, so keep it humid and regularly mist with water.

7 After a week, remove the cutting from the propagator for an hour. If the cutting does not wilt, leave it out for another hour and check again. If it is okay then it probably has sufficient roots to support itself. If it wilts, spray it with water and put it back under the cover for another day before checking again. Once out of the propagator, keep the cutting under the CFL lighting for a few days before moving it to the more powerful HID lights.

POTTING UP

What's that? Pot? I'm afraid not that kind of "pot" just yet; we're talking about the type to put your seedlings in. Potting up is the process of growing a plant in a smaller container and increasing the size in stages, rather than planting directly into the final container, as this can slow down growth and increase the risk of pests and diseases.

Most growers re-pot their plants after about two weeks into 5–6in (125–150mm) pots. Next, when the roots have completely filled that pot (but are not potbound), they transplant to the final pot size—3 liters minimum but 11 liters is typical (6 liters for autoflowering strains). Use plastic containers rather than wood, metal, stone, or ceramic ones as they can contaminate the medium. When potting up to your final size in a soil grow, use square pots rather than round ones as they are more space-efficient.

Anytime a plant is re-potted it causes stress, which can stunt growth for a few days, so don't re-pot once flowering has started. Similarly, owing to the short life of autoflowering strains, it's best to go straight from the starter container to the final pot size.

You will need:

For soil:
- 5–6in (125–150mm) pot
- Soil and perlite
- Gravel or clay pebbles

For hydro:
- 5–6in (125–150mm) net pot and clay pebbles

OR
- Rockwool cube

1 When the seedling is approximately 4in (10cm) tall, with several leaves and plentiful root growth spreading to the edges of the pot, it is ready to be potted up.

2 If growing in soil add a layer of gravel or clay pebbles to the bottom of your new pot to aid drainage. Fill the rest with a mixture of one part perlite to three parts soil, gently pack it down, and water. Make a hole in the soil big enough to fit the small pot inside. Some growers choose to add a root stimulant to the hole at this stage.

3 Gently squeeze and tap the small pot containing the seedling so as to loosen the soil from the pot. Then place your hand on top of the soil with the seedling stem protruding between your middle and fourth fingers.

4 Carefully turn the plant upside-down so it is balanced on the hand holding it, and use the other hand to remove the pot.

5 Now cup the soil and root-mass in both hands, trying to prevent it from breaking apart, and lower it into the hole. Add any extra soil around it to fill the hole, gently pack it down, and tap the sides of the pot so that all the soil settles down inside.

6 If growing in rockwool cubes you should be able to insert the smaller cube into the pre-cut hole of the larger one.

7 If using a net pot of clay pebbles, place the small pot inside the larger one, ensuring there is a layer of pebbles around all sides of the small pot, including above and below.

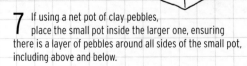

TEMPERATURE AND HUMIDITY

When it comes to temperature, weed plants are a bit like Goldilocks: one minute they are too hot, the next they are too cold. You'll have to keep your eye on that thermometer to make sure the climate in your grow room is just right. The optimum temperature for growing weed is around 70–85°F (20–30°C) when the lights are on and 62–72°F (17–22°C) when they are switched off. Young plants prefer warmer temperatures with relatively high humidity, but as they get older they become more tolerant to colder and drier conditions.

As a rule, colder temperatures slow down growth, especially below 60°F (15°C), while freezing temperatures can shock or kill a plant. Colder temperatures can also encourage some types of mold, especially when damp. Cannabis plants are fairly resistant to heat, but anything above 85°F (30°C) will slow down growth and temperatures exceeding 95°F (35°C) can cause damage. High temperatures can also encourage infection and nutrient burn owing to increased water transpiration.

The temperature difference between lights on and off should not be more than 10°C (5°C is ideal). So if it is 28°C (82°F) with the lights on it should not go below 18°C (64°F) when they are off. This temperature shift affects the internodal length, with a smaller difference resulting in more compact plants and denser buds. During the first 2–3 weeks of flowering, some growers increase the night-time temperature to match the daytime to limit the internodal growth as much as possible, before reducing the night-time temperature back to its original level.

Flowering is the time when temperature is crucial and should be kept relatively low to increase yield and bud size. Reducing the night temperature in the last few weeks of flowering (often while it's being flushed) can also bring out any purple, pink, or blue shades in the buds. During these last few weeks, use a dehumidifier to reduce humidity as much as possible to encourage increased resin production in these final days.

The best way to monitor heat and humidity is with a digital thermometer and hygrometer. The ventilation can then be used to control the conditions with a humidifier/dehumidifier being introduced if further control of the humidity is needed. All strains of cannabis will have varying preferences of temperature and humidity, and it really comes down to experimenting and finding out your own individual requirements. However, the following table will give you an idea of what to aim for at different stages of the grow:

Optimum conditions for different stages of growth

GROWTH STAGE	TEMPERATURE	RELATIVE HUMIDITY
Seedlings and Cuttings	70–77°F (21–25°C)	70–80%
Vegetative Stage	75–82°F (24–28°C)	50–80%
Flowering Stage	65–77°F (18–25°C)	40–50%

As well as the environmental temperature, hydroponic growers also need to monitor their reservoir temperature. The oxygen-retaining capability of water is reduced as it heats up, so maintaining the correct temperature is highly important in order to provide sufficient aeration to the roots. Ideally you want to aim for 65–75°F (18–20°C). As you can see from the following data, a ten-degree rise can greatly reduce the oxygen level:

RESERVOIR TEMPERATURE	DISSOLVED OXYGEN LEVEL
10°C (50°F)	13 parts per million (ppm)
20°C (68°F)	9–10ppm
30°C (86°F)	7ppm

PH

Sadly, pH doesn't stand for pot heads (where would you be on the scale from 1 to 14?), but instead is the measure of how alkaline or acidic a substance is. A scale of 1 to 14 is used, with 1 being the most acidic, 14 the most alkaline, and a pH of 7 being neutral.

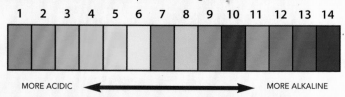

A number of elements are needed by a plant for nutrition—such as nitrogen and potassium—which are obtained through its roots. These various elements are more easily absorbed at differing pH levels, and at some points they can't be absorbed at all, which is known as "nutrient lockout." When this happens, the plant will show signs of deficiency in that element, despite it actually being present.

pH is much less of an issue for soil growers than for those using hydroponics, because the organic matter in soil has natural pH-buffering capabilities. Those growing with pH-balanced soil and using organic nutrients will be unlikely to have any pH problems, and only really need to check if something does go wrong. To measure pH, you will need either a digital pH meter or a pH testing kit. However, these are only suitable for testing liquids, so if growing in soil test the pH of the nutrient solution prior to watering your plants and then test the pH of the "run-off" (the liquid that drains from the pot). The midway point between the two readings is the approximate soil pH.

If a plant is showing signs of nutrient lockout caused by incorrect pH, flush the plants with pure, pH-adjusted water. To do this when using soil, pour twice the volume of the plant pot of water through the soil, wait for five minutes, and repeat. Then feed with only water for a week. Hydroponic growers should drain their systems and replace with water only, before introducing nutrients again after a few days.

Because the different elements are more easily absorbed at varying pH levels, it is best to let your plants experience a varied pH range. For soil aim for a pH of around 6.5–7.0; hydroponic solutions should be around 5.5–6.0 (see tables opposite for a detailed list of optimum pH). You can see from the tables how nutrient availability is affected by pH.

Nutrient lockout charts

SOIL GROW

pH	NITROGEN	PHOSPHORUS	POTASSIUM	MAGNESIUM	CALCIUM	ZINC	IRON	SULPHUR	MANGANESE	BORON	COPPER	MOLYBDENUM
5.0												
5.1												
5.2												
5.3												
5.4												
5.5												
5.6												
5.7												
5.8												
5.9												
6.0												
6.1												
6.2												
6.3												
6.4												
6.5												
6.6												
6.7												
6.8												
6.9												
7.0												
7.1												
7.2												
7.3												
7.4												
7.5												
7.6												
7.7												
7.8												
7.9												
8.0												

HYDRO GROW

pH	NITROGEN	PHOSPHORUS	POTASSIUM	MAGNESIUM	CALCIUM	ZINC	IRON	SULPHUR	MANGANESE	BORON	COPPER	MOLYBDENUM
5.0												
5.1												
5.2												
5.3												
5.4												
5.5												
5.6												
5.7												
5.8												
5.9												
6.0												
6.1												
6.2												
6.3												
6.4												
6.5												
6.6												
6.7												
6.8												
6.9												
7.0												
7.1												
7.2												
7.3												
7.4												
7.5												
7.6												
7.7												
7.8												
7.9												
8.0												

NUTRIENT LOCKOUT ▨   ▨ NUTRIENT BEST AVAILABLE

To use this chart, measure your pH, then look out for any orange boxes indicating elements that may be unavailable to your plant.

> Use products called "pH Up" and "pH Down" to adjust the pH. Don't stir too vigorously before testing, as the extra oxygen can raise the pH. Air pumps have a similar effect, and you should test the pH again after an hour to check for changes.

NUTRIENTS

Imagine going on a date with possibly the fussiest eater imaginable. Now imagine this date lasts for four months. That's what it's like trying to keep your weed plant fed and happy!

Cannabis plants need over 20 elements to grow. Carbon, hydrogen, and oxygen are absorbed from the air and water, while the rest, known as mineral nutrients, are added to the nutrient solution. The three primary nutrients, which are required in the greatest quantities, are nitrogen (N), to promote growth of leaves and vegetation; phosphorus (P), to encourage root and shoot growth; and potassium (K), to regulate water and nutrient movement, and increase flowering and hardiness. When buying plant food, the primary nutrient content (or N-P-K values) will be written on the packaging as three numbers, with each number representing the ratio of these elements.

The secondary nutrients, which are required in smaller amounts, are calcium (Ca) and magnesium (Mg). These are followed, in even smaller quantities, by the trace elements iron (Fe), sulfur (S), manganese (Mn), boron (B), molybdenum (Mo), zinc (Zn), and copper (Cu). Finally, other elements such as aluminum, chlorine, cobalt, iodine, selenium, silicon, sodium, and vanadium are also needed, but in trace amounts that are normally present as impurities in the water or other nutrient products.

Although general-purpose fertilizer can be used, feeds (both chemical and organic) specially designed for cultivating weed are better. Just be sure to follow the manufacturer's instructions.

As a plant grows, it requires the various elements in different amounts. For rooting and germination, high levels of phosphorus with less nitrogen and potassium are needed. During vegetative growth, cannabis plants need lots of nitrogen, plus plenty of phosphorus and potassium, whereas a flowering plant will need less nitrogen and more phosphorus and potassium. For this reason cannabis nutrients are usually labeled for either vegetative or flowering growth.

As well as the main vegetative and flowering nutrients, there are many other additives available, some more beneficial than others. Using just the main nutrients alone will give great results, but as you gain experience you will no doubt experiment with some of these other products and discover what works best for you.

You can tell if your plant is lacking a particular nutrient by visual signs such as the discoloring of leaves or stems. This can often be remedied by using extra feed containing the deficient element, but be careful not to be misled by nutrient lockout caused by an excess of another element (see page 41) or an incorrect pH (see page 40). Adding more nutrients in these cases can actually cause more problems. You can use the table on page 44 to diagnose a nutrient deficiency.

THAT'S DOPE: getting the munchies

Why, after a smoke, do you get the urge to stuff your face with food? It's down to something in the brain called the endocannabinoid system, which consists of naturally occuring cannabinoids and the receptors that they bind to. When your stomach is empty a cannabinoid tells the brain you are hungry by binding to specific receptors. THC is chemically similar to this cannabinoid and binds to these "hunger" receptors, tricking your brain into thinking you need food. It also interacts with receptors in the brain's olfactory bulb, intensifying your sense of taste and smell; as well as in the *nucleus accumbens*, boosting dopamine levels, which makes scoffing food feel so good.

NUTRIENT DEFICIENCIES AND DIAGNOSIS

SYMPTOMS	N	P	K	CA	
Yellow Upper Leaves	No	No	No	No	
Yellow Middle Leaves	No	No	No	No	
Yellow Lower Leaves	Yes	Yes	Yes	No	
Red Stems	Yes	Yes	Yes	No	
Necrosis	No	No	Yes	No	
Spots	No	No	No	No	
Growing Shoots Die	No	No	No	No	
White Leaf Tips	No	No	No	No	
Stunted Growth	Yes	Yes	No	Yes	
Deformed New Growth	No	Yes	No	No	
Yellow Tips	No	No	No	No	
Twisted Growth	No	No	No	No	

Look out for any of the symptoms below: they may be caused by a nutrient deficiency or overfeeding. If your plants show such signs, use this table to identify what nutrients your plant may be lacking.

S	MG	FE	MN	B	MO	ZN	CU	OVER FERT.
Yes	No	Yes	No	No	No	No	No	No
No	No	No	No	No	Yes	No	No	No
No	Yes	No	No	No	No	No	No	No
No	Yes	No	No	No	No	No	No	No
No	Yes	No	Yes	Yes	No	No	Yes	No
No	No	No	Yes	No	No	No	No	No
No	No	No	No	Yes	No	No	No	No
No	Yes	No	No	No	No	Yes	No	No
No	No	No	No	No	No	No	No	No
No	No	No	No	No	No	No	No	No
No	No	No	No	No	No	No	No	Yes
No	No	No	No	Yes	No	No	No	No

WATERING PLANTS

Cannabis plants are snobs: they turn their leaves up at plain old tap water and instead want to drink something a bit more refined. The truth is, tap water can contain a few nasty chemicals, such as chlorine, that your plants won't appreciate, so be sure to dechlorinate it first. Products are available that do this, or simply leave water to stand for 2–3 days and the chlorine will evaporate. You should also establish the pH of your nutrient solution and adjust if necessary (see page 40).

SOIL GROWING

Cuttings and seedlings do not need feeding for the first couple of weeks; just give them water. After that, gradually move them onto the feeding schedule for your chosen nutrient range, ensuring it is one intended for soil use. Knowing when to water your plants is simple: if the pot feels light and the top few inches of soil is dry, water it. If the soil is damp under the surface or it still feels fairly heavy, then leave it a day or so. Overwatering can lead to problems, so make sure plants have ample drainage and are not left to stand in run-off liquid for too long.

Unless your nutrients say otherwise, do not change to flowering feed as soon as you switch to a flowering light cycle. Instead use the vegetative feed until growth has slowed and flowering has begun.

Once a month, give a feeding of just pure water to your plants. This reduces the risk of problems from nutrient build-up. Finally, two weeks before harvest, flush the plants by stopping the supply of nutrients and feeding them with water only until harvest (see page 56).

HYDROPONICS

A very weak nutrient solution can be used for seedlings and cuttings. After that, gradually move onto the schedule for your chosen nutrient range. As with soil growing, don't change to the flowering feed until flowering has begun. Finally, flush the plants one week before harvest.

Regularly check the pH of your reservoir and adjust as required (see page 40). You should also regularly check the nutrient concentration, known as the total dissolved solids (TDS), with an electrical conductivity (EC) meter. This gives the TDS measurement expressed in parts per million (ppm). Water evaporation and absorption by the plants will lower the reservoir water level and can raise the TDS. Top up the reservoir daily, with plain pH-balanced water to lower the TDS back to the desired level or 50 percent strength nutrient solution to raise it. Every two weeks completely drain the reservoir and fill it with a fresh batch of solution. The following shows the recommended TDS and pH levels throughout different stages of a hydroponic grow:

	INDICAS		SATIVAS	
	TDS	pH	TDS	pH
Seedlings/cuttings	300–400ppm	5.3–5.5	250–350ppm	5.3–5.5
Early vegetative	500–600ppm	5.3–5.6	300–500ppm	5.3–5.6
Middle vegetative	600–800ppm	5.4–5.6	500–700ppm	5.4–5.6
Late vegetative	800–1000ppm	5.5–5.7	700–900ppm	5.5–5.7
Early flowering	1000–1300ppm	5.5–5.7	1000–1100ppm	5.5–5.7
Middle flowering	1400–1600ppm	5.5–5.8	1100–1300ppm	5.5–5.8
Late flowering	1000–1100ppm	5.5–5.7	800–1000ppm	5.5–5.7
Ripening	300–500ppm	5.4–5.6	300–500ppm	5.4–5.6

Overfeeding is a common mistake growers make. It is better to give too little than too much—underfeeding may slow growth but overfeeding can be fatal. Healthy plants should generally be a bright shade of green, while very dark leaves are a possible sign of overfeeding. Similarly to lockout from incorrect pH (see page 41), overfeeding some nutrients can lead to others being locked out, giving the impression of a deficiency. Be careful not to confuse the two. To treat, flush the plants as described for a pH lockout (see page 40). The nutrients affected by an excess of other elements can be seen in the table below:

ELEMENT IN EXCESS	ELEMENT AFFECTED	ELEMENT IN EXCESS	ELEMENT AFFECTED
Nitrogen	Potassium, Calcium	Copper	Iron, Molybdenum, Manganese, Zinc
Potassium	Nitrogen, Calcium, Magnesium	Zinc	Iron, Manganese
Phosphorus	Zinc, Iron, Copper,	Molybdenum	Copper, Iron
Calcium	Boron, Magnesium, Phosphorus	Sodium	Potassium, Calcium, Magnesium
Magnesium	Calcium, Potassium	Aluminum	Phosphorus
Iron	Manganese	Ammonium Ion	Calcium, Copper
Manganese	Iron, Molybdenum, Magnesium	Sulfur	Molybdenum

TRAINING

What if I were to say to you that with just a little bit of extra effort and without the need for any magic potions, mystic incantations, or voodoo rituals, you could considerably improve your harvest? Well, my young pot padawan, I'm going to do exactly that.

Although you can grow weed plants wild and free, you may find that a little training can dramatically increase your yield or help control the size and shape of a plant. The main methods used are low stress training (LST) and high stress training (HST). The latter causes physical damage to the plant to get the desired results, so only use it during the vegetative stage, when there is time to recover. For the same reason, this method is not recommended for autoflowering strains.

HOW IT WORKS

Cannabis plants contain hormones called auxins that cause the growth of buds. These auxins are most concentrated at the top of the main central shoot that stretches up toward the light, known as the apical bud. As well as promoting bud growth, the auxins also inhibit bud growth elsewhere on the plant. Removing (or repositioning) the apical bud halts the inhibiting effect, increasing auxin levels elsewhere, resulting in multiple new apical buds.

HIGH STRESS TRAINING (HST) TECHNIQUES

Topping: This is used to increase yield and decrease height. The whole apical bud (or more of the plant) is cut away at a 45-degree angle, causing the two side shoots below to become new apical buds. Topping can be repeated on the new growth, resulting in the development of even more bud sites.

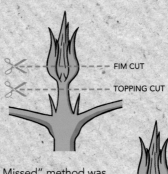

FIM CUT

TOPPING CUT

The FIM Method: The "F**k I Missed" method was stumbled upon by a grower who tried to top a plant, missed, and only removed part of the apical bud. This resulted in several new bud sites rather than the two achieved by topping. To FIM a plant, use sharp scissors to cut about 80 percent from the top of the apical bud. This can be repeated on any new growth.

Lollipopping: For this method of training, lower leaves and side shoots are removed. This does not increase the total yield but it will increase the size of your main buds, eliminate lower "popcorn" buds, and improve air circulation within the plant.

Super Cropping: This involves squeezing and bending the stem into a 90-degree angle, applying enough pressure that you feel a slight cracking in the stem and can fold it over like a kinked hose. This can be repeated on other suitable branches. Over time the bend will heal and the plant will produce auxins in other areas that are exposed to lots of light, resulting in bushy, bud-smothered plants.

STEM BENT AT 90 DEGREES

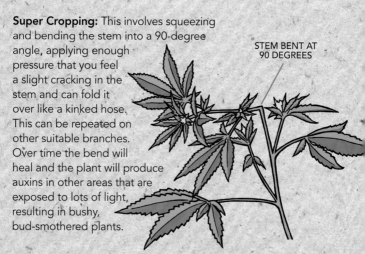

LOW STRESS TRAINING (LST) TECHNIQUES

Bending and Tying: Here, plants are trained to grow horizontally by bending and tying them down using wire or string. Any time the plant is tied down it will grow back toward the light, so regular bending and tying are needed. Like super cropping, this spreads auxin production along the stem, resulting in more bud sites.

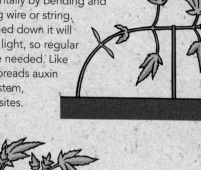

Screen of Green (SCROG)*: This is similar to bending and tying, but the plant is grown beneath a wire screen. As the plant grows, it is bent down and tied to the screen, resulting in a dense, shallow canopy of buds. SCROG is usually combined with lollipopping and topping/FIMming.

* Don't confuse with Sea of Green (SOG), which is a method for growing lots of miniature plants packed together to create a dense but short layer of foliage.

PESTS AND DISEASES

As a weed smoker, your number one enemy was most likely to be the cops busting your sorry ass for lighting up in public. Don't get me wrong, the police are still to be avoided at all costs, but the biggest threat to your plants is now from a smaller, but just as irritating group: bugs, and their accomplices fungi and bacteria. These little bastards get everywhere, so be extra vigilant because prevention is always easier and more effective than treatment. If you do happen to get affected, I've recommended some chemical treatments in the following pages, which are available from garden centers, grow shops, or online.

Grow rooms and equipment should always be kept clean and tidy. Grow your plants at optimum temperatures in a contained space with ample ventilation. Never use equipment that was previously used outside unless it has been sterilized, don't reuse soil, and always sterilize reusable hydroponic mediums and other equipment between uses.

PESTS—IDENTIFYING AND TREATING

Aphids: Usually gray or black but can vary in color. They remain stationary while sucking nutritional liquid from any area of a plant. To make matters worse, while tucking into your precious crops these aphids exude a sticky honeydew, which attracts ants.

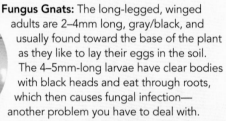

Physical Treatment: Remove small infestations from your plants by hand. Use sticky traps to catch aphids and other bugs.

Chemical Treatment: Insecticidal soap, pyrethrum (aerosol).

Fungus Gnats: The long-legged, winged adults are 2–4mm long, gray/black, and usually found toward the base of the plant as they like to lay their eggs in the soil. The 4–5mm-long larvae have clear bodies with black heads and eat through roots, which then causes fungal infection—another problem you have to deal with.

Physical Treatment: Encouraged by humidity and damp soil, so provide ample ventilation and do not overwater.

Chemical Treatment: Bacillus thuringiensis var. israelensis (Bti) for adult gnats. Neem oil or insecticidal soap soil drench to kill larvae.

Leaf Miner Maggots: Despite having a pretty cool name, these are tiny maggots that burrow through leaf matter. As they munch your plants, they leave behind a telltale white outline of their tunnel, so you know you've been messed with.

Physical Treatment: Crush the visible maggots inside their tunnels and remove severely infested leaves.

Chemical Treatment: Water plants with a 0.5 percent solution of neem oil.

Spider Mites: The most common pest for indoor growers, these tiny eight-legged critters live underneath the leaves and suck out liquid. Look out for the yellowish-white spots they leave stippled on the tops of the leaves. The two-spotted mite is most common, but red and yellow-white varieties are also found.

Physical Treatment: Treat small infestations by reducing temperature to 60°F (16°C) and blasting the mites off with cold water. Remove leaves with more than 50 percent damage. After infestation, fully clean the grow room with 5 percent bleach solution.

Chemical Treatment: Neem oil, pyrethrum, horticultural oil, or insecticidal soap. Spider-mite eggs hatch in 5–10 days, so use two or three applications at 5–10-day intervals to kill them all.

Thrips: Tiny winged insects about 1–1.5mm long. They tend to move in groups, making them easier to spot. Whitish-yellow specks are left behind on top of leaves, which can darken and crumble from lack of chlorophyll.

Physical Treatment: Manual removal is possible, but they can be difficult to catch.

Chemical Treatment: Pyrethrum or insecticidal soap sprayed 2–4 times at 5–10-day intervals.

White Flies: Can be detected by shaking a branch and seeing if they fly out from the leaves. Like mites, they suck from the plant, leaving behind white stipples and signs of diminished chlorophyll.

Physical Treatment: None.

Chemical Treatment: Spray with natural sprays, insecticidal soap, or pyrethrum. Before spraying remove any leaves with over 50 percent damage and then apply spray at 5–10-day intervals.

FUNGI, VIRUSES, AND BACTERIA

Botrytis, also known as gray mold, is a bluish-gray hairlike fungus that starts within the buds and can even affect harvested weed. To prevent it, keep buds dry, maintain less than 50 percent humidity, and provide sufficient ventilation. If harvested, fully dry and cure before storing (see page 56).

Downy mildew appears as whitish-yellow spots on top of leaves with bumps of mycelium spores opposite on the underside. Spreading rapidly, it causes a lack of vigor and slows growth with leaves turning yellow and dying.

Powdery mildew exhibits itself as little bumps on top of the leaves which develop into a pale, powdery coating. It can be prevented with the use of high light levels, low humidity, and a plentiful air supply.

Root rot causes roots to turn from white to brown. Leaves show signs of chlorophyll depletion followed by wilting and slowed growth. It is most common when roots are stood in un-aerated water for a long time.

Damping off (*also known as Pythium wilt*) is a fungal condition that is usually brought on by damp soil. It attacks seedlings and cuttings, causing them to lose girth, weaken, wilt, and die.

Viruses and bacteria can also attack cannabis plants. Signs include spots, blotches, or swirling patterns on leaves, sickly growth, yellowing, wilting, low yields, and death.

TREATING FUNGI, VIRUSES, AND BACTERIA

Remove any infected plants form the grow room. Bordeaux mixture is an effective treatment for many fungal conditions, but there are no biological or chemical treatments for viruses. Consuming infected weed can be bad for your health, so unfortunately, if a problem is too wide spread, you may need to destroy the whole plant.

HARVESTING, DRYING, AND CURING

Finally, at long last, the time you've been patiently waiting for has arrived. You've not been this excited since you were a kid waiting for Santa to show up on Christmas morning. So what are you waiting for? Clear the decks and get those scissors ready!

Cannabis plants are best harvested when their buds are at full ripeness, and there will be a window of 5–7 days in which to do this. Around 1–3 weeks before peak ripeness, a plant's growth will slow and its pistils will darken. But the best way to determine harvest time is by studying the trichomes with a pocket microscope. Their bulbous heads start off clear and colorless, ripening to a cloudy appearance as the THC increases, before turning amber or brown as the THC decays. By observing the rate of change, you can predict the optimum harvest and flush times. Harvest when all the trichomes are mostly cloudy, with a few starting to turn amber.

Tetrahydrocannabinol (THC) gives you the uplifting and cerebral "high" feeling, while another cannabinoid, called cannabidiol (CBD), provides the physically relaxing "stoned" feeling. As the trichomes darken, the THC decays and is converted into cannabinol (CBN), which causes the uneasy sensations a user may feel. When this change happens it makes the effects of the CBD more prominent. Some growers will delay harvest to get a more sedating weed, but this is really just a waste of THC. For a particular high, you should instead select a strain that naturally peaks at a certain level of THC and CBD.

Drying is important, as it causes decarboxylation (see page 67) and prevents weed from going moldy when it's stored. Once dried, the buds can be cured, evenly distributing any remaining moisture, enhancing taste, and increasing aroma.

HOW TO HARVEST, DRY, AND CURE

1 Flush your plants two weeks before harvest. Pour lots of water through the growing medium, wait a few minutes, and repeat. Feed with water only for the final weeks, stopping three days before harvest. Turn off all lights for the final 24 hours and reduce humidity to boost resin production. Harsh-tasting starches and sugars build up in foliage during the day but are stored in the roots at night, so cut the entire plant down or cut all the branches off while it is still in the dark.

2 Cut off any of the larger leaves that aren't covered in many trichomes.

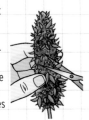

3 Now cut or pull away all the sugar leaves—the smaller, more resinous ones. Remove them close to the stem or just trim them in line with the edge of the bud. Keep any trimmings, as they can be used for making hash (see pages 58-65) or for cooking (see pages 66-79).

4 The plants now need to be dried. This is usually done by hanging the branches on strings. For best results dry in the dark, with good ventilation, at 65-75°F (18-24°C) and a humidity of 45-55 percent. Check daily for mold. Some people prefer to swap stages 3 and 4, in what is known as a dry trim, as they find it improves taste and aroma.

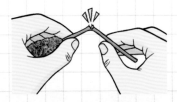

5 It should take 5-7 days to dry enough for curing. Check by bending some stems: if the stem snaps it is ready to be cured, if it just flexes then it needs longer.

6 To cure the buds, cut them from the branches and put them in an airtight container. Any remaining moisture will evenly spread through the buds as they "sweat" in the container. Open for ten minutes every 4-5 hours so fresh air can get in. If they feel noticeably moist after sweating, leave them out for a few hours to crisp up.

7 After a couple of weeks the buds will have cured fully and will be ready for using or storing. They will be about 25 percent of their original weight. Store your weed in a refrigerator or a cool, dark place.

MAKING HASH

If your past experiences of hash were smoking a jet-black, rock-hard lump of something that tasted like burning rubber, then you're in for a treat. The often misunderstood world of hashish includes some of the purest, most potent forms of cannabis available, and is worlds apart from the cheap "rocky" that you smoked as a teenager and burnt holes in your parents' sofa.

Hash is made by separating the resin glands (trichomes) from the plant matter and binding them together, usually with heat and pressure. The heat and pressure also improve the potency through decarboxylation (see page 67). THC levels can be much higher in hash than in weed—up to 75 percent in hash and over 90 percent in hash oil, compared to 10–25 percent in weed. Hash making dates back thousands of years, rubbing and pressing being the two traditional techniques used. More recently the knowledge gained from these has been used to develop modern techniques such as ice-water and chemical extraction.

RUBBED HASH is made by rubbing hands over fresh flower buds until they become coated with sticky resin, which is then collected up into a ball. As the ball is rubbed and warmed, the trichome heads burst and the THC oxidizes, giving the outside a dark brown or black color.

PRESSED HASH is produced by shaking dried buds over a mesh screen to separate off the trichomes, which are then pressed, sometimes with heat, to form a solid block. A finer mesh and briefer shaking will allow less vegetable matter through, resulting in a higher grade of hash.

CHEMICAL EXTRACTION is used to make hash oil. The cannabis is mixed with a solvent, such as isopropyl alcohol or butane, which dissolves the resin. This solution is then filtered to remove the plant matter before the solvent is evaporated, leaving behind the hash, which can be viscous like oil or solid and shatterable like glass.

ICE-WATER EXTRACTION is done by agitating weed in ice and water. The freezing temperature makes the trichomes brittle and easy to break away from the foliage. The oil-based trichomes will not dissolve in water and, being heavier than water, will sink, whereas the water-soluble material dissolves and the foliage floats. The trichomes can then be extracted and pressed into hash known as "iceolator." It is also called

"bubble hash" because of the way it bubbles when a flame is held to it—the higher the purity, the more bubbles there are.

ICE-WATER EXTRACTION BAGS

In 1998 Mila Jansen, owner of the Pollinator Company in Amsterdam, invented a system for ice-water extraction using a specially designed set of bags which she called "Ice-O-Lator Bags." These consisted of three nylon bags with progressively smaller micron screens sewn into the bottom of each.

This method was then developed further by a Canadian known as Bubble Man. He added more bags with even finer screens (to separate the hash into more grades), and in 1999 he released his range, called Bubble Bags.

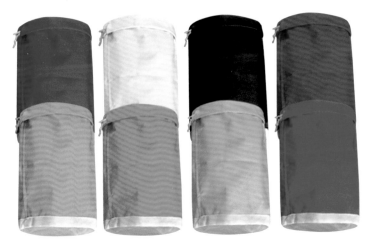

MAKING BUBBLE HASH WITH EXTRACTION BAGS

"If it don't bubble, it ain't worth the trouble," is a well-known saying among hash connoisseurs—and believe me, get yourself some of these bags and you will be able to make some incredi-bubble hash. And the best part is that you can make it from the trimmings left over from harvest.

You will need:

- Set of ice-water extraction bags and appropriate size bucket
- Cold water
- Enough ice for your size of bags/bucket
- Broken up buds or trimmings that have been frozen while still fresh and undried
- Wooden spoon or handheld mixer with paddle attachment
- Metal spoon
- Pressing/blotting screen
- Thermometer

NB: Using as much weed as possible is not necessarily a good thing. The following maximum weights of weed are recommended for each size of bag:
1 gal—2oz/56g
5 gal—8oz/200g
20 gal—32oz/1000g

1 Place the bags inside each other so the bag with the largest screen size (the "work bag") is innermost and the screens get progressively smaller. Put the bags into the bucket.

2 Add some water and ice, half of the weed, more ice, the remaining weed, and top up with more ice and water. Stir so it is all mixed up and leave to stand until the temperature of the mixture gets to 39°F (4°C) or lower. Some people recommend using RO (reverse osmosis) water, a purer form of water that is available from aquarium shops.

3 Stir the mixture with the wooden spoon for 15 minutes to break the trichome heads from the weed. You can use a mixer but it will break up the weed more and lead to a lower-quality hash.

4 Let it sit for 15 minutes so that the trichome heads can settle through the screens. Then pull out the work bag, letting the water drain out. If any resin glands are stuck to the underside of the screen, rinse them off into the next bag.

5 Let the water sit for 30 minutes then pull out the second bag. You will see a layer of wet trichomes on the screen inside. Use the metal spoon to scrape it up and spread it onto the pressing screen.

6 Repeat for any remaining bags. Sandwich the resin within the screen and press out some of the moisture with paper towels. Leave out for a day or so to dry fully. It can then be crumbled and smoked straight away or pressed into a block.

Don't throw away the wet weed when you have finished. You can use it for a second ice-water extraction, a chemical extraction (see page 64), or making cannabis-infused ingredients (see page 68). Your plants will also love being fed the nutrient-rich leftover water.

MAKING BUBBLE HASH IN A JAR

If you're a bit of a cheapskate or have spent all your cash on growing equipment, channel your inner MacGyver and use an old jar and a coffee filter to mimic the effects of a bubble bag and make epic hash.

You will need:

- Large mason jar or similar
- Broken-up buds or trimmings that have been frozen while still fresh and undried
- Cold water
- Ice cubes
- Draining spoon and normal spoon
- Kitchen strainer (sieve) and a container for it to sit on
- 1 or 2 large paper coffee filters
- Baking tray or pressing/blotting screen

1 Fill the jar to about halfway with your weed, top up with ice cubes, and fill almost to the top with water.

2 Screw on the lid, shake for 10 minutes to break the trichome heads from the plant matter, then put in the fridge for 30 minutes.

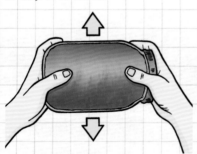

3 The weed will have floated to the top and a layer of trichome heads will have settled to the bottom. Use the draining spoon to scoop out all the weed.

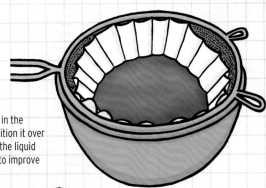

4 Place a coffee filter in the strainer (sieve), position it over the container, and drain the liquid through (use two filters to improve the purity).

5 The coffee filter will be coated in wet resin. Use a spoon to push it toward the center of the filter, then close it up and gently squeeze out some of the water.

6 Open out the filter, scrape up the hash and spread it onto the baking tray or screen. Leave to dry for a day or so. It can then be crumbled up to smoke straight away or pressed into a block.

Don't throw away the wet weed when you have finished. You can use it for a second ice-water extraction, a chemical extraction (see page 64) or making cannabis infused ingredients (see page 68). Your plants will also love being fed the nutrient rich leftover water.

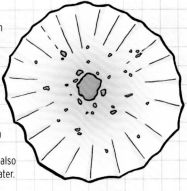

MAKING ISO HASH

After drinking their own bodyweight in beer and then hitting a packed bong, many people find alcohol and weed don't mix very well. However, they are actually the perfect pairing when it comes to making ISO hash—a chemically extracted hash oil made using isopropyl alcohol. It is also called QWISO hash, which stands for quick wash isopropyl hash, "quick wash" referring to the short time the weed is in the alcohol.

You will need:

- Mason jar or similar
- Buds or trimmings that have been dried, crumbled, and frozen overnight
- Isopropyl alcohol, ideally 99 percent purity, but if not, use anything over 91 percent
- 2 kitchen strainers (sieves) and two containers that they will fit over
- Large paper coffee filters
- 1 or more flat-bottomed glass dishes
- Desk fan
- Single-sided razor blade or similar

1 Add your weed to the jar, cover with isopropyl alcohol, and leave to stand for 30 seconds.

2 Shake the jar vigorously for 30 seconds. Any longer and you will begin dissolving chlorophyll and other substances in the plant matter.

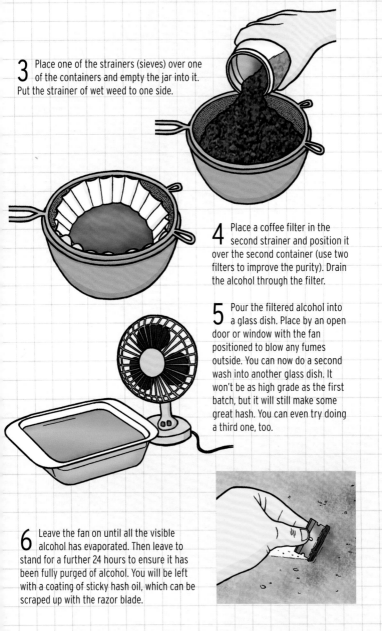

3 Place one of the strainers (sieves) over one of the containers and empty the jar into it. Put the strainer of wet weed to one side.

4 Place a coffee filter in the second strainer and position it over the second container (use two filters to improve the purity). Drain the alcohol through the filter.

5 Pour the filtered alcohol into a glass dish. Place by an open door or window with the fan positioned to blow any fumes outside. You can now do a second wash into another glass dish. It won't be as high grade as the first batch, but it will still make some great hash. You can even try doing a third one, too.

6 Leave the fan on until all the visible alcohol has evaporated. Then leave to stand for a further 24 hours to ensure it has been fully purged of alcohol. You will be left with a coating of sticky hash oil, which can be scraped up with the razor blade.

COOKING WITH WEED

You've successfully grown and harvested your first crop of sticky, sweet buds, and maybe even made some ultra-potent hash too, but what's the best way to enjoy the fruits of your labor? A key thing to consider is the temperature to which your cannabis is heated, because anywhere above 315°F (157°C) and you begin to lose cannabinoids (the good stuff). A joint can contain as little as 10 percent of the potential THC, while a bong will give you around 40 percent. A vaporizer is a better option, providing a potential THC hit of anywhere from 50 percent up to 95 percent, and without the harmful combustion by-products like carbon monoxide that you get with a joint or bong. The Volcano vaporizer (right) is widely considered to be the best on the market, with superior build quality and exceptional performance. In all forms of smoking and vaporization, though, as much as 30–40 percent of the inhaled THC is lost when the vapor is exhaled.

WHY EAT YOUR WEED?

By far the healthiest and most efficient way to absorb cannabinoids is to eat or drink them, which ensures that 100 percent of them enter your body. However, the rate of absorption is much slower than when inhaled, usually taking 30–90 minutes to have an effect. The high also lasts considerably longer, with effects sometimes as long as ten hours. If you are unsure of the potency, eat a small amount and wait a couple hours before eating any more. If you do end up having a bad trip, try drinking the juice from fruits containing citric acid, such as orange or grapefruit, to reduce the effects. Eating pistachios or pine nuts can also help, as both contain pinene, a chemical that improves mental clarity.

Weed shouldn't just be eaten raw, as there are some properties that are brought on by heat. The THC present in raw weed is in its non-psychoactive form, tetrahydrocannabinolic acid (THCA). At 115–122°F (46–50°C) it begins releasing carbon dioxide and converts into its psychoactive form, tetrahydrocannabinol (THC). This reaction is known as decarboxylation.

To be readily absorbed by the body, cannabinoids must first be dissolved. As they are lipophilic (can be dissolved in fats and oils), people usually extract the cannabinoids into butter, vegetable oil, or milk. These can be used, even when cold, to make cannabis-infused food and drink, referred to as "edibles."

The cannabinoids are also soluble in alcohol, so "tinctures" can be made by extracting cannabinoids into drinks with a high alcohol content. However, cannabinoids are insoluble in water. This is why brewing cannabis tea is not very effective unless the drink is combined with milk.

One final point: the serving quantities provided are suggestions only and will vary depending on the strength of the canna butter/oil/milk and your personal tolerance levels. Go easy at first, it's better to use too little than too much.

HOW TO MAKE
CANNA BUTTER AND OIL

Right, you must have developed quite an appetite with all the work you've put into growing your weed, so now it's time to cook up some tasty treats. The key ingredient to most cannabis-infused recipes is canna butter or oil, which can even be made from the trimmings left over from harvest.

You will need:

- 2–4oz (50–100g) weed trimmings or 1–2oz (25–50g) buds, dried and ground (quantities can be varied to suit personal preference)
- Baking tray
- Aluminum foil
- Oven thermometer
- Large pan
- 3 pints (1.5 liters) water
- 16oz (450g) butter or 2 pints (1 liter) vegetable oil
- Cheesecloth (muslin) and kitchen strainer (sieve)
- 2 large containers
- 4 tbsp soy lecithin powder/granules (optional)

1 Before you make the canna butter, the THC in the weed must undergo a process called decarboxylation (see page 67). To do this, preheat the oven to 220-240°F (104-116°C/gas mark 1). Keep the temperature within this range and never let it exceed 300°F (150°C/gas mark 2). Spread the weed out on a baking tray and cover with foil, loosely but sealed tightly around the tray. Put into the oven for 30 minutes. Leave to cool fully before opening the foil, to prevent vapor loss.

2 Heat up the water in the pan, add the butter or oil and weed, stir, and bring to the boil. Reduce to a very low heat, put the lid on, and simmer for 2-3 hours, stirring occasionally.

3 Fold the cheesecloth (muslin) into a double layer, place in the strainer (sieve) and put that into a large container. Pour the mixture through.

4 Once all the liquid has drained through, bundle up the wet weed inside the cheesecloth and squeeze out as much remaining liquid as possible.

5 If using butter, put the container into the refrigerator. After a while the water and butter will separate, with a layer of butter solidifying on top of the water. Once separated, discard the water.

If using oil, leave the mixture out for 1-2 hours so the oil and water separate. Then put it in the freezer for 4-6 hours so the water freezes and you can pour off the oil. If the oil has coagulated in the freezer, scrape it off. It will liquefy at room temperature.

6 The butter or oil can be used as it is, but it can be further improved with the introduction of lecithin. When added, it will make the effects of the cannabis come on much faster and feel a lot stronger. Gently melt or warm the canna butter or oil in a pan, stir in the lecithin until it dissolves, then pour the butter or oil back into the storage container. This will keep for about a month, or longer if frozen. Use it in place of some, or all, of the butter or oil in any recipes.

TO MAKE CANNA MILK

Replace the butter or oil with milk and don't add water. As no water has been added, no subsequent separation is required.

WAKE AND BAKE
BANANA PANCAKES

Wakey, wakey! Rise and shine! It's a beautiful day you're missing out on! What's that? Your head's a bit groggy? I'm not surprised, with the amount of weed you smoked last night! Never fear, I've got just the thing for you: Wake and Bake Banana Pancakes! They're the tasty way of getting your breakfast buzz back on. These are small, American-style pancakes made with nutritious bananas and a generous helping of canna milk to set you up for the day!

METHOD

• In a mixing bowl, mash up the banana with a fork really well so it becomes a smooth paste.

• Sift the flour and baking powder into the bowl.

• Add the egg, milk, and melted butter, if using. Thoroughly mix, using an electric mixer if possible, so that it becomes creamy and aerated. For oaty pancakes you can swap some of the flour with an equal quantity of oatmeal.

• Warm a frying pan over a medium heat. When sufficiently hot, melt a little butter in the pan. Then spoon or pour in enough batter to make a pancake about 4in (10cm) wide. Fill up any more space in the pan with pancakes, being careful not to let them spread into each other.

• When bubbles start appearing on the surface of a pancake, flip it over with a spatula and cook for another minute or so on the other side.

• When sufficiently cooked on both sides, remove from the pan and carry on cooking more pancakes with the remaining batter.

• Serve with maple syrup at breakfast time or enjoy with ice cream for a dank dessert!

Ingredients

• 1 over-ripe banana
• 1 cup (4oz/120g) all-purpose (plain) flour
• 1 tsp baking powder
• 1 egg
• ¼ pint (140ml) canna milk
• 1oz (25g) butter or canna butter, melted (optional)
• butter, for frying

Makes 12 pancakes

CINNAMON DOPE-NUTS

You might think that cops and stoners don't have much in common, especially if you've ever had the misfortune of getting busted smoking or growing a bit of weed. Well, you're right for the most part, they don't usually see eye-to-eye, and cops should be avoided at all costs. However, one bond that we do share is a love for sweet and unhealthy food–especially donuts! So keep a stash of these handy, and if you're ever unlucky enough to have your rights read, offer some to the boys in blue and hopefully they'll soon be too baked to remember why they turned up in the first place.

METHOD

• Preheat the oven to 350°F (180°C/gas mark 4). Spray or grease two 6-hole donut pans well.

• Sift the dry ingredients together into a large bowl. Melt the canna butter in another bowl in a microwave and then add the egg, milk, and vanilla. Then whisk it all together. Pour this mixture into the dry ingredients and stir until it's all combined.

• Pour the batter into the donut pans so each hole is about three-quarters full. Bake in the oven for 15–20 minutes. They are ready when you poke them with a knife and it comes out clean.

• While the dope-nuts are cooling, make the coating. Mix the sugar and cinnamon together in a bowl then melt the remaining butter in a pan. Now dunk each dope-nut in the melted butter and roll it in the sugar and cinnamon.

Ingredients

• 2 cups (9oz/250g) all-purpose (plain) flour
• 1½ cups (10½oz/300g) superfine (caster) sugar
• 2 tsp baking powder
• 1 tsp ground cinnamon
• ½ tsp ground nutmeg
• ½ tsp salt
• 1oz (30g) canna butter
• 1 large egg
• 10fl oz (300ml) full-fat (whole) milk
• 2 tsp vanilla extract

For the coating:

• ½ cup (3½oz/100g) sugar
• ½ tsp ground cinnamon
• 4oz (120g) canna butter

Makes 12 dope-nuts

PEANUT SHATTER

Be very, very careful... this is the most fragile cannabis confectionery you will ever eat. This nutty toffee treat pays homage to butane honey oil, also known as BHO or "shatter," the most potent type of hash there is. Not everyone can get their hands on real shatter, but with this recipe you can have the next best thing. So cook up a batch and handle with care, because both this delicate delicacy and your mind are about to get shattered!

METHOD

• Grease or line a large baking sheet, preheat the oven to 400°F (200°C/gas mark 6), and put the sheet in to warm.

• Place the sugar, corn (golden) syrup, and water in a large pan and bring to a boil over a medium heat, stirring frequently so it doesn't burn.

• Mix in the peanuts and heat until the temperature reaches 300°F (150°C). This will take about 15 minutes.

• Remove the baking sheet from the oven.

• Stir the canna butter into the toffee until it has melted. Remove from the heat and immediately mix in the baking powder.

• Pour the mixture into the tray, spreading it all the way to the edges with two forks.

• Leave to cool completely, at least 1 hour, before shattering into pieces ready to be devoured.

Ingredients

• 1½ cups (10½oz/300g) sugar
• 8fl oz (225ml) corn (golden) syrup
• 8fl oz (225ml) water
• 16oz (450g) honey-roasted peanuts (or any other nuts)
• 3 tbsp canna butter
• 1½ tsp baking powder
• cooking/candy thermometer

Serves 6–10

CARAMEL AND CASHEW CANNA COOKIES

Forget "more-ish," these cookies are downright addictive! They're so alluringly packed with the perfect pairing of salted cashew nuts and sticky caramel pieces, you won't be able to put the cookie jar down. Just be careful that one bite doesn't lead to you scoffing the whole lot, though, as they are loaded with potent canna butter and will leave you more baked than the inside of your oven. These irresistible edibles are definitely not a good idea for work tea breaks!

METHOD

• Preheat the oven to 350°F (180°C/gas mark 4) and grease or line two large baking sheets.

• Roughly break up the cashew nuts.

• In a mixing bowl, cream together the butter and sugars.

• In a separate bowl, lightly beat the egg. Add to the creamed butter and sugar along with the vanilla and mix together.

• Sift in the flour, salt, and bicarbonate of soda and mix together.

• Add the chopped caramels and cashew nuts to the dough and mix in.

• Roll the dough into balls about 2in (5cm) wide and flatten slightly onto the baking sheets. Don't pack the cookies in too close together as they do spread out a lot when cooking.

• Bake in the oven for 8 minutes for a really gooey cookie or up to 14 minutes for a slightly crisper one. They may seem undercooked, but they will harden considerably as they cool.

Ingredients

• 3½oz (100g) salted cashews
• 3½oz (100g) caramels. If you can't get caramel pieces, cut up some larger caramel candies or even slice up chocolate-coated caramel bars.
• 4oz (125g) softened canna butter
• ½ cup (3½oz/100g) soft light brown sugar
• ½ cup (3½oz/100g) superfine (caster) sugar
• 1 egg
• 1 tsp vanilla extract
• 1¾ cups (8oz/225g) all-purpose (plain) flour
• 2 tsp salt
• ½ tsp bicarbonate of soda

Makes 12–18 cookies

CARAMEL PECAN POT-CORN

We're off to the movies! Ever since the release of the unintentionally hilarious anti-weed film *Reefer Madness* in 1936, cannabis culture and cinema have gone hand in hand. The ground-breaking *Easy Rider*, smoking Labrador with Cheech and Chong, rolling a Camberwell Carrot in *Withnail & I*, f**king up the rotation with Smokey in *Friday*, the Dude in *The Big Lebowski*, the back of a twenty-dollar bill (…on weed!) in *Half Baked*, getting the munchies for White Castle with *Harold & Kumar*, and cross-joints of Pineapple Express… and what better way to enjoy these canna classics than by rolling a fat joint of home-grown and tucking into a bowl of sticky, nutty, pot-laden popcorn!

METHOD

• In a large pan, heat the vegetable oil and add the popcorn kernels. Put a lid on the pan and cook for 3–4 minutes. Shake the pan occasionally until the popping stops and then transfer to a large bowl.

• Wipe the pan clean with a cloth. Dice the canna butter and add it to the pan along with the sugar and honey. Heat gently, stirring all the time, until the sugar has completely dissolved.

• Bring to the boil and bubble rapidly, without stirring, for 4–5 minutes. The mixture will be ready when it has turned a caramel color.

• Add the popcorn and chopped pecans and thoroughly stir until all the popcorn is coated in caramel and nuts.

• Empty the pan onto a couple of non-stick baking sheets and leave to cool. Once cooled and hardened, break up into pieces and serve in a bowl.

Ingredients

• 2 tbsp vegetable oil
• 7oz (200g) popcorn kernels
• 4oz (125g) canna butter
• ¾ cup (5oz/150g) superfine (caster) sugar
• 2 tbsp clear honey
• ¾ cup (3½oz/100g) chopped pecans

Serves 2–4

MARSHMALLOW BROWNIES

No weed cookbook would be complete without a brownie. The originator of all the culinary cannabis creations that have been concocted since, it deservedly earns its place in the history books as well as the cookbooks. But with the brownie well into its golden years, it's the perfect time to give it a bit of a makeover. So, what better way to make the stoner's favorite even greater than by topping it with melted marshmallows and more chocolate!

METHOD

• Preheat the oven to 350°F (180°C/gas mark 4) and line or grease a 9x13in (23x33cm) baking tray.

• In a large bowl, cream together the sugar, butter, cocoa powder, and vanilla.

• In a separate bowl, lightly beat the eggs and add to the mixture. Sift in the flour and baking powder and mix thoroughly.

• When mixed, stir in the white chocolate chunks. Make the chunks reasonably large so they don't melt away in the oven.

• Pour the mixture into the prepared tray, spreading it all the way into the corners. Bake in the oven for 25–30 minutes, until the top looks cooked.

• Remove from the oven and cover the top of the brownie with a blanket of marshmallows, then sprinkle the chocolate chips on top.

• Return to the oven for a few minutes so the marshmallows melt slightly and begin to turn brown.

• It will be really hot and sticky, so resist the temptation to dive straight in; instead leave it to cool fully before taking out of the tray and cutting into pieces.

Ingredients

• 2 cups (14oz/400g) sugar
• 8oz (225g) canna butter, melted
• 2½oz (60g) unsweetened cocoa powder
• 1 tsp vanilla extract
• 4 eggs
• 1¾ cups (8oz/225g) all-purpose (plain) flour
• ½ tsp baking powder
• ½ cup (3½oz/100g) white chocolate chunks
• 7oz (200g) mini white marshmallows
• ½ cup (3½oz/100g) milk chocolate chips

Makes 18 brownies

RASTA PASTA

Put on a Bob Marley album, light up the chalice, and "pass the kouchie pon de left hand side," because it's time to pay homage to the Rastafari movement, a way of life that has become synonymous with weed and cannabis culture. This recipe fuses Italian and Jamaican influences by combining cheesy pasta with jerk chicken. Red peppers, green peppers, and golden corn are added to represent the famous Rasta colors, then of course the all-important ingredient–plenty of ganja to make you feel irie!

METHOD

• Put all the marinade ingredients into a food processor and blitz until smooth. Place the chopped chicken breasts in a dish and smother with the marinade. Cover with plastic wrap (cling film)and refrigerate for at least an hour (overnight if you can wait that long).

• Bring a large pan of water to a boil (this will be for the pasta): Meanwhile, melt the butter in another pan, add the flour, and stir until it forms a smooth paste. Then pour in the milk, stirring well with a hand whisk.

• Put the marinated chicken into a frying pan and cook over a medium heat until browned. Add the chopped peppers and corn to the frying pan and continue to cook over a medium heat.

• Tip the pasta into the boiling water and cook as per the packet's instructions.

• Meanwhile, slowly bring the sauce to a boil, stirring continuously until it thickens. Remove from the heat and stir in the cheese.

• When the pasta is ready, the chicken is fully cooked, and the peppers are soft, drain the pasta and mix them all together, ready to be served.

For the jerk marinade:

• 5oz (150g) chopped onion
• 1 scotch bonnet or other chile, deseeded and chopped
• 1oz (30g) fresh ginger, peeled and chopped
• ½ tsp ground allspice
• a few sprigs fresh thyme, leaves only
• ½ tsp ground black pepper
• 3fl oz (75ml) white wine vinegar
• 3fl oz (75ml) dark soy sauce

• 4 chicken breasts, chopped
• 2oz (50g) butter (or canna butter for extra potency)
• ½ cup (2oz/50g) all-purpose (plain) flour
• 1 pint (500ml) canna milk
• 1 red bell pepper, chopped
• 1 green bell pepper, chopped
• 3½oz (100g) canned corn kernels
• 10½oz (300g) pasta
• 4oz (120g) grated cheese

Serves 4

STONED BAKED PIZZA

You've heard of the Leaning Tower of Pisa, but what about the "lean power of pizza"?! Well, when it comes to food that gets you high, this Italian-inspired snack can't be topped. This is the perfect party food for slicing up and sharing with hungry stoner friends, and as both the base and the sauce are made using potent canna oil, it's probably a good thing if you don't scoff it all by yourself!

For the sauce:

- 14oz (400g) canned chopped plum tomatoes
- 3 tbsp tomato paste
- 3½fl oz (100ml) canna oil
- 2 garlic cloves, minced
- ½ tbsp dried basil
- ½ tbsp dried oregano
- ½ tbsp chili powder
- ½ tsp salt
- ½ tsp ground black pepper

- 10fl oz (300ml) warm water
- 1 sachet fast-action dried yeast
- 1 tbsp sugar
- 3 tbsp canna oil
- 3 cups (13oz/375g) all-purpose (plain) flour, plus extra for dusting
- 1 tsp dried thyme
- 1 tsp salt
- 2 large handfuls grated mozzarella

Makes 2 pizzas

METHOD

- Put all the sauce ingredients into a pan and cook over a medium heat, stirring well. Bring to a gentle boil, then lower the heat and simmer for 30 minutes, stirring occasionally. Remove from the heat, transfer to a bowl, and refrigerate for a couple hours before using.

- To make the pizza base, mix the water, yeast, sugar, and oil in a bowl. Add the flour, thyme, and salt. Mix and knead for 10–12 minutes, sprinkling with flour to stop it sticking to the bowl.

- The dough should be elastic and smooth. Place it in an oiled bowl, drizzle with some more oil, cover with plastic wrap (cling film), and leave to stand for an hour.

- Separate the dough into two halves and roll them into balls. Cover with a damp dish towel and leave to stand for another 10 minutes. Preheat the oven to 400°F (200°C/gas mark 6).

- Roll the dough out onto two pizza pans or stones and poke some holes in it with a fork to let steam escape while cooking. Now all that's left is to smother your pizza bases with the special tomato sauce, sprinkle on some grated mozzarella cheese, and add any of your favorite toppings, if you like. Bake in the oven for about 20 minutes.

GROOVY SMOOTHIES AND HAZY SHAKES

After all this cooking in a hot kitchen you've no doubt got a thirst to quench. Luckily canna cooking isn't just limited to candy, cakes, and dinners; by brewing up a batch of weed-infused milk (see page 69) you can make some cool and refreshing shakes and smoothies. They're perfect for washing down some other THC treats or soothing your throat after a big hit on the bong. If you're after a health kick, the smoothies both contain two of your five fruit or veg a day, and surely the weed counts as a third one… doesn't it?!

METHOD

• To make these delicious drinks, simply whizz all the ingredients together in a blender. Each one will serve two people.

Banana, Kiwi, and Ginger Smoothie

• 9fl oz (250ml) canna milk
• 1 banana, peeled and sliced
• 1 kiwi fruit
• handful of ice
• 1 tbsp honey
• 1 tsp vanilla extract
• 1in (2.5cm) piece finely grated ginger

Strawberry and Cinnamon Smoothie

• 9fl oz (250ml) canna milk
• 1 banana
• 5 strawberries
• handful of ice
• 1–2 tsp ground cinnamon

Quadruple Chocolate Milkshake

• 9fl oz (250ml) canna milk
• 2 tbsp chocolate syrup
• 1 tbsp unsweetened cocoa powder
• 1 pint (500ml) chocolate ice cream
• your favorite chocolate bar, chopped into pieces

Cookies and Cream Milkshake

• 9fl oz (250ml) canna milk
• 1 pint (500ml) vanilla ice cream
• 1 tsp vanilla extract
• 8 Oreo cookies, broken into pieces

GANJA GUACAMOLE AND SKUNK SALSA

Hola amigos! It's time to turn the heat up in here and get a bit spicy! From Mexican Rudy and Acapulco Gold to Cheech and Chong, "La Cucaracha," and even the word "marihuana," Mexico and cannabis have a long history together. So don't siesta, let's fiesta by piling up some tortilla chips and smothering them in Skunk Salsa and Ganja Guacamole, plus a dash of sour cream and some sliced jalapeño peppers to finish it off.

Ganja Guacamole

- 3 ripe avocados, halved, with stones removed
- 1 ripe tomato, chopped
- 1 small red onion, finely chopped
- 1 chile, deseeded and finely chopped
- handful of cilantro (coriander), chopped
- juice of 1 lime
- 2 tbsp canna oil
- salt and black pepper

METHOD

- Scoop out the flesh of the avocados into a bowl, then add the tomato, onion, chile, and cilantro (coriander). Add the lime juice and canna oil, and season with salt and pepper.

- Use a fork to mash it all up until it gets to your preferred consistency.

Skunk Salsa

- 4 ripe tomatoes, chopped
- ¼ red onion, chopped
- ¼ red bell pepper, chopped
- handful of cilantro (coriander), chopped
- 3 garlic cloves, minced
- 1 jalapeño pepper, finely chopped
- juice of 1 lime
- 4 tbsp canna oil
- salt and black pepper

METHOD

- Mix all the ingredients in a bowl and season with salt and pepper. Toss thoroughly and leave to stand for 30 minutes before serving.

INDEX